Unseen Poetry

Exam Board: AQA

Poetry can be blindingly beautiful, especially if you're seeing it for the first time. In fact, it can be difficult to compose yourself and write an equally beautiful essay about the poem in an exam.

But don't panic. This CGP book is a fantastic way to make sure you're ready. It's packed with everything you'll need to get a top grade — sample poems, worked examples, practice questions, full answers and exam advice.

Once you've worked through all that, you'll have no problem handling any poems the examiners throw at you!

GCSE English
The Poetry Guide

Book One

Published by CGP

Editors:
Siân Butler
Eleanor Claringbold
Rachel Craig-McFeely
Catherine Heygate
Matt Topping
Jennifer Underwood

With thanks to Claire Boulter for the proofreading.
With thanks to Emily Smith for the copyright research.

ISBN: 978 1 78294 364 8
Printed by Elanders Ltd, Newcastle upon Tyne.
Clipart from Corel®

Based on the classic CGP style created by Richard Parsons.

Contents

What You Have to do in the Exam

As part of your **AQA English Literature** course, you'll have to sit **two exams**.
This book will help you prepare for the **Unseen Poetry** questions, which are in **Paper 2**.

This is how your Paper 2 exam will work

1) The Paper 2 exam lasts for **2 hours and 15 minutes**. It will be split into **three sections** like this:

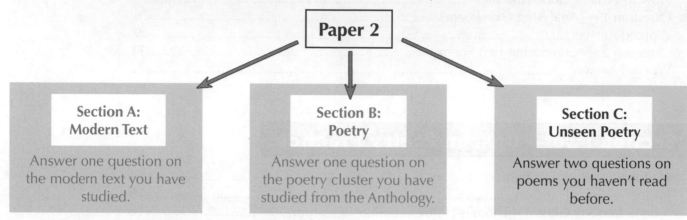

Paper 2

Section A: Modern Text

Answer one question on the modern text you have studied.

Section B: Poetry

Answer one question on the poetry cluster you have studied from the Anthology.

Section C: Unseen Poetry

Answer two questions on poems you haven't read before.

2) For **Section C** you will be given **two poems** that you haven't read before and will have to answer **two questions** about them.

3) In the exam, you should spend about **45 minutes** answering the questions in **Section C**.

You will have to answer two questions about the unseen poems

1) **Question 1** is worth **24 marks** and will ask you to analyse **one poem**. Your answer should cover:

- **What** the poem is **about** — the poem's **message**, **themes** and **ideas**.
- **How** the poet uses **form**, **structure** and **language** to **communicate** these ideas.

2) For **Question 2** you'll have to **compare both poems**. This question is worth **8 marks**.

3) You should write about **similarities** and **differences** between the two poems. Your answer to this question must focus on the **techniques** the poets use, such as **form**, **structure** and **language**.

4) Question 1 is worth **a lot more marks** than Question 2, so in the exam make sure you spend **more time** on your answer to **Question 1**.

The examiner is looking for four main things

To **impress the examiner** with your answers to the questions in Section C, you need to:

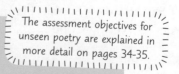

The assessment objectives for unseen poetry are explained in more detail on pages 34-35.

1) Show that you **understand** what the poems are **about**.
2) Write about the **techniques** used in the poems.
3) **Support** every point you make with **quotes** or **examples** from the poems.
4) Use the **correct technical terms** to describe the techniques used in the poems.

Five Steps to Analysing the Unseen Poems

The following three pages will explain the **main things** that you need to do to **get to grips** with poems that you haven't seen before. Think about them as the pathway to **Unseen Poetry** glory — how exciting.

Follow these five steps to analyse unseen poems

There are **five main steps** that you need to follow to **analyse** and **write about** a poem you've never seen:

1) Work out **what the poem's about** — you need to identify its **subject** and **voice**.
2) Identify the **purpose, theme** or **message** — work out the **overall message** of the poem before you start to analyse it in more depth.
3) Explore the **emotions, moods** or **feelings** in the poem — e.g. is the poem positive or gloomy?
4) **Identify** the **techniques** used in the poem — think about the **language, form** and **structure**. Think about **how** the poet uses these techniques to **create meaning** and affect the **reader**.
5) Give a **personal response** — make sure to include **your thoughts** and **feelings** about the poem.

Don't try to look for **all** of the features the **first time** you read through the poem.

Instead, **read** the poem over a **few times**, working through each of the steps **in turn** — this will help you get a **clearer understanding** of the poem and keep your analysis **focused** and **relevant** when you start writing.

1) Work out what the poem's about

1) Work out the **subject** of the poem.
E.g. "The poem is about the narrator's relationship with his parents".
2) Look at whether it's written in the **first** person ("I"), **second** person ("you") or **third** person ("he / she / they").
3) The poem's **voice** can have a big **effect** on how its subject is conveyed — e.g. a **first-person** voice can make the poem sound **personal**, as if the narrator is expressing their **private thoughts**.
4) Think about **who** the poem is **addressing**, e.g. the narrator's lover or the reader.

Pick out the important bits of the poem as you read it — underline them or make notes.

2) Identify the purpose, theme or message

1) Think about **what** the poet is saying, **why** they've written the poem, or what **ideas** they're using.
2) The poem could be an **emotional response** to something. It might aim to **get a response** from the **reader**, or put across a message or an opinion about something.
3) There could be **more than one** purpose, theme or message in the poem — e.g. a poem might be written to **entertain**, but also to **inform** the reader about an important issue.

3) Explore the emotions, moods or feelings

1) Think about the **different emotions or feelings** in the poem.
2) Identify the poem's **mood** or **atmosphere** — think about **how** the poet has created a certain atmosphere in the poem with language, structure and form (see step 4).
3) Look out for any sudden **changes** in the mood — they could **highlight** an **important idea** in the poem.
4) Make sure that anything you say about mood and emotions is **relevant** to your argument.
5) Don't forget to **explain** the **effect** of the poem's mood on the reader.

Five Steps to Analysing the Unseen Poems

4) Pick out the techniques used in the poem

1) Think about the **different techniques** the poet has used to create the **emotions**, **moods** or **feelings** in the poem. Make sure you use the correct **technical terms** when you write about these techniques.

2) Comment on **why** the poet has used these techniques, and what **effect** they create.

3) **Don't** just **list** the poetic techniques used — choose examples that are **relevant** to your argument.

Identify the poem's form and structure

1) **Form** refers to features such as the **type of poem**, the number and length of **lines** and **stanzas**, **rhyme scheme** and **rhythm**.

Don't worry if you don't know what type of poem it is — focus on whether the poem's form is regular or irregular, and if aspects of form change throughout the poem.

2) Here are some **common elements** of form to look out for:

Type	Features
Blank verse	• iambic pentameter • no rhyme scheme
Dramatic monologue	• first-person narrator • addresses an implied audience
Free verse	• no rhyme scheme • irregular rhythm and line lengths
Sonnet	• 14 lines • regular rhyme scheme • often uses iambic pentameter • usually used for love poetry

Rhyme	Features
Alternating (ABAB)	• 1st and 3rd lines rhyme • 2nd and 4th lines rhyme
Half-rhymes	• Words that have a similar, but not identical, end sound, e.g. "<u>shade</u>" and "<u>said</u>"
Internal rhyme	• Two or more words rhyme, but at least one of them isn't at the end of the line, e.g. "<u>the **beat** of a horse's **feet**</u>"
Rhyming couplet	• A pair of rhyming lines that are next to each other

Rhythm	Features
Iambic pentameter	• 10 syllables per line, alternating between an unstressed and a stressed syllable
Iambic tetrameter	• 8 syllables per line, alternating between an unstressed and a stressed syllable

3) **Don't** just **identify** the poem's form — think about **why** a particular aspect of form has been used. Consider the **effect** it creates and how it helps to convey the poem's **central ideas**.

4) **Structure** is about **how ideas progress** through the poem and any **changes** in mood or **tone**. Look at how the poem **begins** and **ends**, and how the poem's message **develops**.

Think about language and imagery

1) Analyse the **language** — think about **why** the poet has chosen certain **words** and **language techniques**.

2) Look out for different types of **imagery** — language that creates a **picture in your mind**:

- **Personification** — describing a **nonliving thing** as if it has **human thoughts** and **feelings**, or **behaves** in a human way.
- **Metaphors** — describing things by saying that **they are something else**.
- **Similes** — describing things by **comparing** them to something else, usually using the words "like" or "as".

3) **Think about** the **effect** of the language and imagery on the reader — consider how it makes you **feel**.

Five Steps to Analysing the Unseen Poems

Look out for poetic devices

1) Poets use **poetic devices** for **effect** in their writing — here are some **examples**, but there are **lots more**:

- **Punctuation** (e.g. caesurae, enjambment, end-stopped lines) affects the poem's **pace** and how it **flows**.
- **Repetition** often **reinforces** a key point or idea.
- **Contrasts** can **emphasise** key ideas or create a **sense of balance**.
- **Sound effects** (e.g. onomatopoeia, sibilance, alliteration, assonance) can create a particular mood or **atmosphere**, **highlight** important ideas or **reflect events** in the poem.
- **Appeals to the senses** create a **vivid** impression by engaging different senses.

Look up any terms you don't know in the glossary at the back of this book.

2) As with everything you pick out of a poem, it's **really important** that you don't just say what the technique is — you also need to **comment** on the **effect** that it has.

5) Include your thoughts and feelings about the poem

1) Examiners love to hear what **you think** of a poem and how it makes **you feel** — giving a **personal response** will make your answer **original** and help it to **stand out** from the crowd.

2) Think about how well the poem gets its **message** across and what **impact** it has on you.

3) Try **not** to use "**I**" though. Don't say "I felt sad that the narrator's brother died" — it's much **better** to say "It makes the reader feel the narrator's sense of sadness at the death of his brother."

4) Think about any **other ways** that the poem could be **interpreted** — if a poem is a bit **ambiguous**, or you think that a particular line or phrase could have several **different meanings**, then **say so**.

Take your analysis further to get a grade 9

There's no single way to get **top marks**, but these points can help take your analysis to the **next level**:

1) Treat the poem as a **conscious creation** — every **word** or **technique** has been **deliberately chosen** by the poet. Show that you understand this by writing about what the **poet** does and **why**:

- **Think carefully** about the poem and analyse in **real depth** the ways the poet creates meaning.
- Pick out **individual words** and **phrases** that are rich in meaning, then explore their **effect** in detail.
- Consider whether there could be **different interpretations** of the poem and comment on them.

2) Develop a **clear argument** and **build your essay** around it. **Link** each paragraph of your answer to your **argument** so that you really **answer the question** in the exam.

3) Remember that the examiners value **quality over quantity** — make a few **highly detailed** and **relevant** points, rather than attempting to write about the whole poem.

Always think about how the poem affects the reader...

It might seem impressive to reel off a list of all the features that you've spotted, but the examiner wants to see whether you can analyse *how* the poet uses these techniques to create meaning and affect the reader.

6

How to Write a Good Answer

It's not just *what* you write, it's *how* you write it. These pages will help you to tick all the examiner's boxes.

Read each question carefully and plan your answers

1) Make sure that you're **familiar** with the **format** of the two **questions**. For **Question 1**, you have to **analyse** one unseen poem, and **Question 2** asks you to **compare** that poem with another one.

2) **Read the questions** carefully — **underline** the **key words** and refer back to them as you write.

3) **Get to grips** with the poem and get a sense of its **message** and **key features** before planning your answer.

4) Write a **short plan** that covers your main points (see **page 9** for more on planning).

Get to the point straight away in your introduction

1) Your **introduction** should begin by **clearly** laying out your **answer** to the question in a sentence or two.

2) Try to use **words** or **phrases** from the **question** in your introduction — this will show the examiner that you're **answering the question**.

3) Use the rest of the introduction to give a **brief overview** of how the poem or poems present the **theme** given in the question — include the **main ideas** from your **plan**, but **save** the **evidence** for later.

4) Keep your introduction nice and **short** — most of your **marks** will come from the **main body** of the essay.

Use the main body of your essay to develop your argument

1) The **main body** of your essay should be roughly three to five paragraphs that **develop** your argument.

2) Make sure each of your points is **linked** to the question and follows a **clear** central **argument**.

3) A good way to do this is to start each paragraph with a **clear point** or **opening statement** that directly connects the poem or poems back to the question.

4) You can use P.E.E.D. to structure your paragraphs. **P.E.E.D.** stands for: **P**oint, **E**xample, **E**xplain, **D**evelop.

POINT — Begin each paragraph by making a **point**.
EXAMPLE — Then give an **example** from the poem.
EXPLAIN — Explain **how** the example **supports** your opening point.
DEVELOP — Finish the paragraph by **developing** your point further.

This is just a framework — you don't have to follow P.E.E.D. rigidly in every paragraph.

5) You can develop your points in a **variety** of ways — here are some ideas:

- **Explain** the **effect** on the reader.
- **Analyse** the **language** more closely.
- **Link** to **another part** of the poem.
- Give an **alternative interpretation** of your example.

6) **Question 2** is a **comparison** question, so your answer needs to be structured differently to Question 1:

- You could **compare** the poems in **each paragraph** by writing about a **feature** of **one poem** and **explaining** how the **other poem** is similar or different.
- Alternatively, you could write about **one poem at a time** — you could write about different elements of **one poem**, then write about **the other**, **comparing** it with the first poem.

Section One — Exam Advice

How to Write a Good Answer

Use details from the text to back up your points

1) You need to **back up your ideas** with **quotes** from or **references** to the poems. Here are some **tips**:

- **Choose** your quotes **carefully** — they have to be **relevant** to the point you're making.
- **Don't** quote **large chunks** of text — keep quotes **short** and cut out anything unnecessary.
- **Embed** quotes into your sentences — this means **placing** them **smoothly** and **naturally** into your writing, e.g. 'The poet describes how the "<u>lost village</u>" lives in the woman's "<u>memory</u>".'
- **Explain** your quotes — you need to use them as **evidence** to support your **argument**.

2) Here's an **example** of how to **use quotes** in your answers, and what to **avoid**:

> ✗ The narrator suggests that her grandmother surrounded herself with objects in the absence of close relationships — "She watched her own reflection in the brass / Salvers and silver bowls, as if to prove / Polish was all, there was no need of love".
>
> ✓ In 'My Grandmother', the narrator suggests that her grandmother replaced her family's "love" with "Polish" — in the absence of loving relationships, she surrounded herself with antiques.

This quote is too long and it doesn't fit into the sentence structure.

These quotes are nicely embedded into the sentence.

3) **Quotes** are usually the **clearest** way to illustrate a point, but sometimes you can use a **paraphrased detail** instead — e.g. if you need to describe one of the **writer's techniques** or one of the **poem's features**.

4) **Don't** write a **lengthy explanation** of what happens in the poem — keep any references **brief** and **relevant**.

Use sophisticated language and relevant technical terms

1) Your writing has to sound **sophisticated** and **stylish**. It should be **concise** and **accurate**, with no **vague words** or **waffle**.

2) You should use an **impressive range** of **vocabulary**. Don't keep using the **same word** to describe something — instead, try to **vary** how you say things.

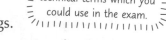 Use the glossary at the back of this book to learn technical terms which you could use in the exam.

3) To get top marks, you need to use the **correct technical terms** when you're writing about poetry.

4) However, make sure you **only** use words that you know the **meaning** of. For example, don't say that a poem has a '**volta**' if you don't know what it **really means** — it will be **obvious** to the examiner.

5) It's **not enough** to just **name** a feature — you need to explain the **effect** that it has on the reader.

Your conclusion must answer the question

1) **Finish** each essay with a **conclusion** — this should **summarise** your **answer** to the question.

2) It's also your **last chance** to **impress** the examiner, so make your final sentence **memorable**. You could **develop** your **opinion** of the poem(s), or **highlight** the **features** that best **support** your argument.

 EXAM TIP

Support your arguments with quotes and examples...

In your essays, it's really important that you back up every point you make with evidence from the poems. As you're analysing the poems, look out for key quotes that you'll be able to use to support your arguments.

Question 1 — Analysing One Poem

The first question will ask you to analyse one of the unseen poems. **Read** the question carefully and underline the **key words**, then **annotate** the poem to pick out the important bits. Here's an example...

Here's a sample exam Question 1

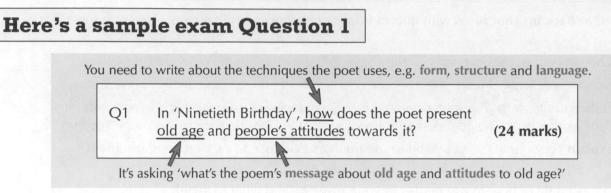

You need to write about the techniques the poet uses, e.g. **form**, **structure** and **language**.

Q1 In 'Ninetieth Birthday', <u>how</u> does the poet present <u>old age</u> and <u>people's attitudes</u> towards it? **(24 marks)**

It's asking 'what's the poem's **message** about **old age** and **attitudes** to old age?'

This is how you might annotate the first poem

Annotate your poem in any way that works for you — underline, highlight or scribble notes.

Read through the poem, and **mark** any bits of it that **stand out**.
Jot down your thoughts too — it'll help you **plan** your essay (see p.9).

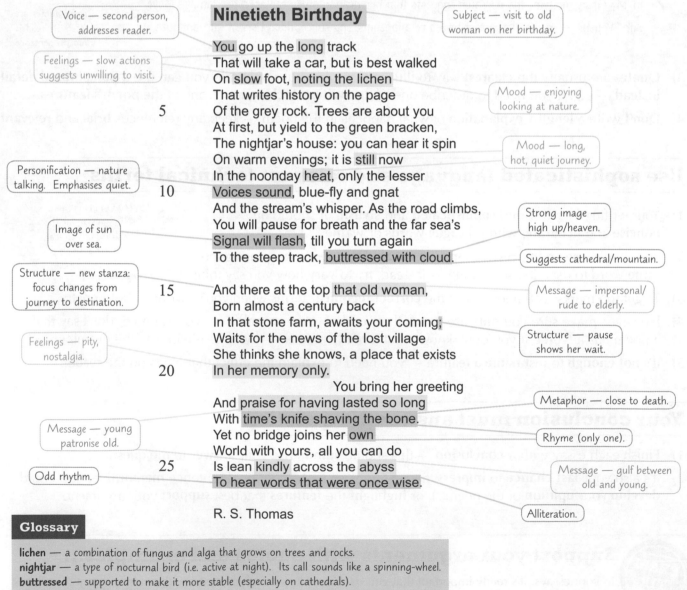

Ninetieth Birthday

Voice — second person, addresses reader.

Subject — visit to old woman on her birthday.

You go up the long track
That will take a car, but is best walked
On slow foot, noting the lichen
That writes history on the page
5 Of the grey rock. Trees are about you
At first, but yield to the green bracken,
The nightjar's house: you can hear it spin
On warm evenings; it is still now
In the noonday heat, only the lesser
10 Voices sound, blue-fly and gnat
And the stream's whisper. As the road climbs,
You will pause for breath and the far sea's
Signal will flash, till you turn again
To the steep track, buttressed with cloud.

15 And there at the top that old woman,
Born almost a century back
In that stone farm, awaits your coming;
Waits for the news of the lost village
She thinks she knows, a place that exists
20 In her memory only.
                    You bring her greeting
And praise for having lasted so long
With time's knife shaving the bone.
Yet no bridge joins her own
World with yours, all you can do
25 Is lean kindly across the abyss
To hear words that were once wise.

R. S. Thomas

Feelings — slow actions suggests unwilling to visit.

Mood — enjoying looking at nature.

Mood — long, hot, quiet journey.

Personification — nature talking. Emphasises quiet.

Image of sun over sea.

Strong image — high up/heaven.

Suggests cathedral/mountain.

Structure — new stanza: focus changes from journey to destination.

Message — impersonal/ rude to elderly.

Feelings — pity, nostalgia.

Structure — pause shows her wait.

Metaphor — close to death.

Message — young patronise old.

Rhyme (only one).

Odd rhythm.

Message — gulf between old and young.

Alliteration.

Glossary

lichen — a combination of fungus and alga that grows on trees and rocks.
nightjar — a type of nocturnal bird (i.e. active at night). Its call sounds like a spinning-wheel.
buttressed — supported to make it more stable (especially on cathedrals).
abyss — a bottomless pit.

Worked Answer

So, you've **read** the poem and have some **ideas** about how you might answer the **question**. The next step is to turn your scribblings into an **essay plan**.

Spend five minutes planning your answer

1) Always **plan** your answer **before** you start — that way, you're less likely to forget something **important**.
2) Focus on **three or four key quotes** from the poem.
3) Remember to write about **what** the poet says and **how** they say it.
4) **Don't** spend **too long** on your plan. It's only **rough work**, so you don't need to write in full sentences.

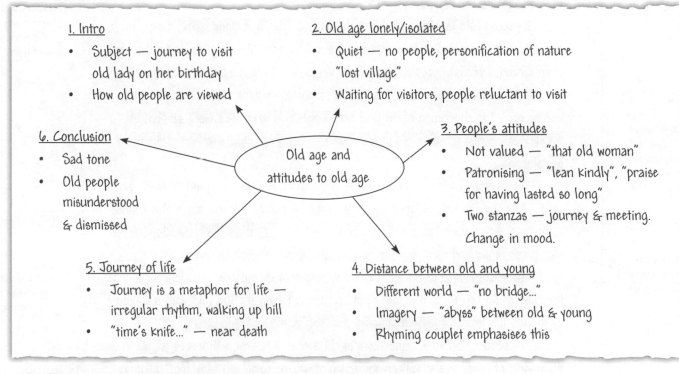

1. Intro
- Subject — journey to visit old lady on her birthday
- How old people are viewed

2. Old age lonely/isolated
- Quiet — no people, personification of nature
- "lost village"
- Waiting for visitors, people reluctant to visit

Old age and attitudes to old age

3. People's attitudes
- Not valued — "that old woman"
- Patronising — "lean kindly", "praise for having lasted so long"
- Two stanzas — journey & meeting. Change in mood.

4. Distance between old and young
- Different world — "no bridge..."
- Imagery — "abyss" between old & young
- Rhyming couplet emphasises this

5. Journey of life
- Journey is a metaphor for life — irregular rhythm, walking up hill
- "time's knife..." — near death

6. Conclusion
- Sad tone
- Old people misunderstood & dismissed

5) Now you've got a **plan** for your essay, you just need to **write** the thing, but today's your lucky day, because I've done this one for you...

This is how you could answer Question 1

Use your essay plan to make sure you answer the question.

> The poem 'Ninetieth Birthday' tackles the issue of old age and the generation gap through a description of a journey to meet an old lady. It raises issues that make you think about old age and how old people are viewed by younger generations. The poem shows how lonely and isolated old age can be. The journey is up a "long track": the old lady is isolated from the real world. She isn't named, which may show that the poem is a general comment on old age, or may reflect her anonymity and lack of importance for most people. The village is described as the "lost village" because she has no contact with people and real life any more. It is "a place that exists / In her memory only", meaning that it has changed so much that the place she knew no longer exists, so her history is lost.

Clear start, mentioning the subject and the main themes of the poem.

Write about the poem's main messages early on in your essay.

Always use quotes to back up points.

This answer continues on page 10.

Worked Answer

Write about feelings and mood, and use quotes to back up your points.

The isolation of old age is also shown through the lack of visitors — the narrator is only visiting because it is her birthday. The only other life mentioned is nature; there's the sound of insects, "Voices sound, blue-fly and gnat" and "you can hear [the nightjar] spin". This suggests that she has no human contact, but the fact that she "awaits your coming" and "Waits for the news", suggests that she is eager for visitors. The use of the words "awaits" and "waits" shows her patience, but also her frustration as the world leaves her behind.

Mention specific language features and explain why the poet used them.

By using cold language like "that old woman" and "that stone farm", the poem emphasises distance and sounds impersonal and uncaring. The language is patronising when talking about how people speak of this woman — there is irony in our "praise" for her "having lasted so long", and "lean kindly" suggests we think we are being kind by visiting her. The alliteration of the final line, "words that were once wise", emphasises the lack of interest shown in old people's views, although it could also hint at the onset of dementia.

Think about different interpretations to help you get top marks.

The personification of nature in the first stanza — "Voices sound, blue-fly and gnat / And the stream's whisper" — reflects the silence of old age, but it also sounds disturbing, with the sibilance adding a secretive tone. "Time's knife" is really effective as a harsh-sounding metaphor for how the old woman is near to death.

Mention any poetic devices that you spot.

The poem is also using a metaphor to comment on old age. The journey along the road could represent the journey of life. On reaching the top (old age) it's almost as though the traveller is going towards heaven, "buttressed with cloud".

Write about any imagery in the poem.

The poem's rhythm is reminiscent of old age — it is slow, with lots of pauses in the middle of lines. It also reflects the action of walking uphill, on "slow foot", pausing for breath. The caesurae make you pause: "In that stone farm, awaits your coming", gets across the old lady's longing for company and her patient waiting. There's hardly any rhyme in the poem, but when there is, it's a couplet that emphasises that there's "no bridge" between the old and young, the past and the present — neither can relate to the other.

Think about the techniques the poet uses to back up the poem's message.

Comment on form and the effect it has.

The message about old age is that the journey of life is hard and can end in loneliness. This is shown through the use of natural imagery, which suggests how isolated the old woman is, and through the attitude of the narrator, who reveals how people feel about the older generation. The poem cleverly puts across how the young and old don't understand each other, and makes the reader question their own attitude towards growing old.

Sum up the <u>what</u> and <u>how</u> in your final paragraph.

Give a personal response to the poem.

Always proofread your answers...

The examiner won't be very impressed if your answers are full of spelling mistakes and grammatical errors, so make sure you leave a couple of minutes at the end of the exam to check through your work.

Question 2 — Comparing Two Poems

Whew, that's Question 1 over and done with. Now it's time to tackle **Question 2**.
I'd have a nice cup of tea and a biscuit first if I were you.

Question 2 will ask you about two poems

1) **Question 2** will ask you to **compare** the **two unseen poems**. This means that you need to write about the **similarities** and **differences** between them.

2) This question is about the **techniques** the poets use and their **effect on the reader**, so focus on the **structure**, **form** and **language** used in the two poems.

3) Remember, Question 2 is **only** worth **8 marks**, so **don't spend too long** on your answer — you just need to make **three or four** clear points and back them up with **examples** from the poems.

Four steps to answering Question 2

- **Don't** be tempted to start writing **without thinking** about what you're going to say.

- Instead, use this handy **four-step plan** to quickly **organise your thoughts** and write an answer that'll knock the examiner's socks off:

  1) **Read** the question carefully and underline the **key words**.

  2) **Annotate** the second poem, focusing on the **techniques** used and how they **affect the reader** (see pages 3-5). Think about **similarities and differences** between these techniques and those used in the first poem.

  3) **Plan** your answer. Identify **three or four** key **similarities and/or differences** that you are going to write about.

  4) **Write** your answer. Use your plan to make sure that **every paragraph** discusses **one similarity or difference** between the **techniques** used in the two poems.

Here's a sample exam Question 2

Before you start annotating the second poem, **read** the question carefully and make sure that you **understand** exactly what you're being asked to do.

Q2   'Ninetieth Birthday' and 'My Grandmother' both explore <u>relationships between young people and the elderly</u>. <u>Compare</u> the <u>methods</u> the poets use to present these relationships.   **(8 marks)**

This is the **theme**.

You need to **compare** the poets' techniques, e.g. **form**, **structure** and **language**, in the two poems.

Make sure you answer the question...

It might sound obvious, but you won't get any marks for writing things that aren't relevant, no matter how brilliant they are. So always read the question and underline the key words before you do anything else.

Worked Answer

Once you're sure you understand the question, you need to get to grips with the **second unseen poem**. Then you'll be ready to **plan** your answer...

This is how you might annotate the second poem

Read through the poem, and **mark** the most important bits. Remember, in your essay you need to write about the **form**, **structure** and **language** used in the poem and the **effect** they have on the reader.

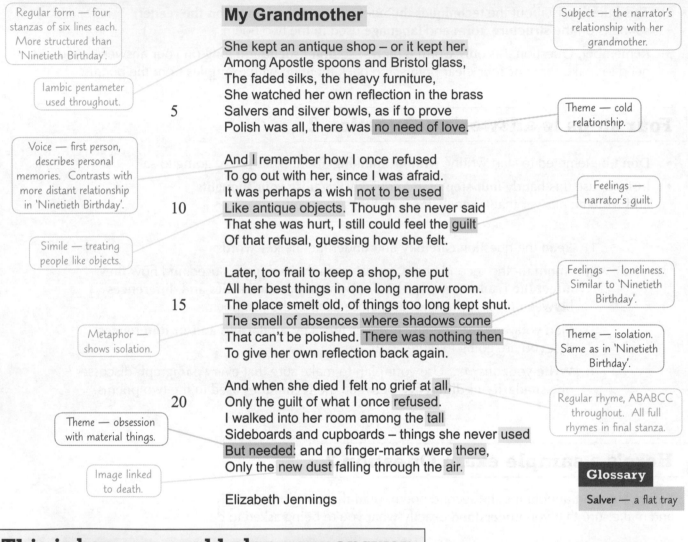

Regular form — four stanzas of six lines each. More structured than 'Ninetieth Birthday'.

Iambic pentameter used throughout.

Voice — first person, describes personal memories. Contrasts with more distant relationship in 'Ninetieth Birthday'.

Simile — treating people like objects.

Metaphor — shows isolation.

Theme — obsession with material things.

Image linked to death.

My Grandmother

She kept an antique shop – or it kept her.
Among Apostle spoons and Bristol glass,
The faded silks, the heavy furniture,
She watched her own reflection in the brass
5   Salvers and silver bowls, as if to prove
Polish was all, there was no need of love.

And I remember how I once refused
To go out with her, since I was afraid.
It was perhaps a wish not to be used
10 Like antique objects. Though she never said
That she was hurt, I still could feel the guilt
Of that refusal, guessing how she felt.

Later, too frail to keep a shop, she put
All her best things in one long narrow room.
15 The place smelt old, of things too long kept shut.
The smell of absences where shadows come
That can't be polished. There was nothing then
To give her own reflection back again.

And when she died I felt no grief at all,
20 Only the guilt of what I once refused.
I walked into her room among the tall
Sideboards and cupboards – things she never used
But needed: and no finger-marks were there,
Only the new dust falling through the air.

Elizabeth Jennings

Subject — the narrator's relationship with her grandmother.

Theme — cold relationship.

Feelings — narrator's guilt.

Feelings — loneliness. Similar to 'Ninetieth Birthday'.

Theme — isolation. Same as in 'Ninetieth Birthday'.

Regular rhyme, ABABCC throughout. All full rhymes in final stanza.

Glossary

Salver — a flat tray

This is how you could plan your answer

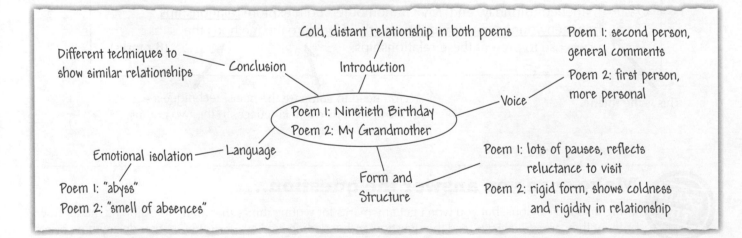

Different techniques to show similar relationships — Conclusion

Cold, distant relationship in both poems — Introduction

Poem 1: second person, general comments

Poem 2: first person, more personal

Voice

Poem 1: Ninetieth Birthday
Poem 2: My Grandmother

Emotional isolation — Language

Poem 1: "abyss"
Poem 2: "smell of absences"

Form and Structure

Poem 1: lots of pauses, reflects reluctance to visit

Poem 2: rigid form, shows coldness and rigidity in relationship

Worked Answer

So, you've **read** the question, you've **annotated** the second poem and you've made a cunning **plan**.
All you need to do now is **write** your **essay**...

This is how you could answer Question 2

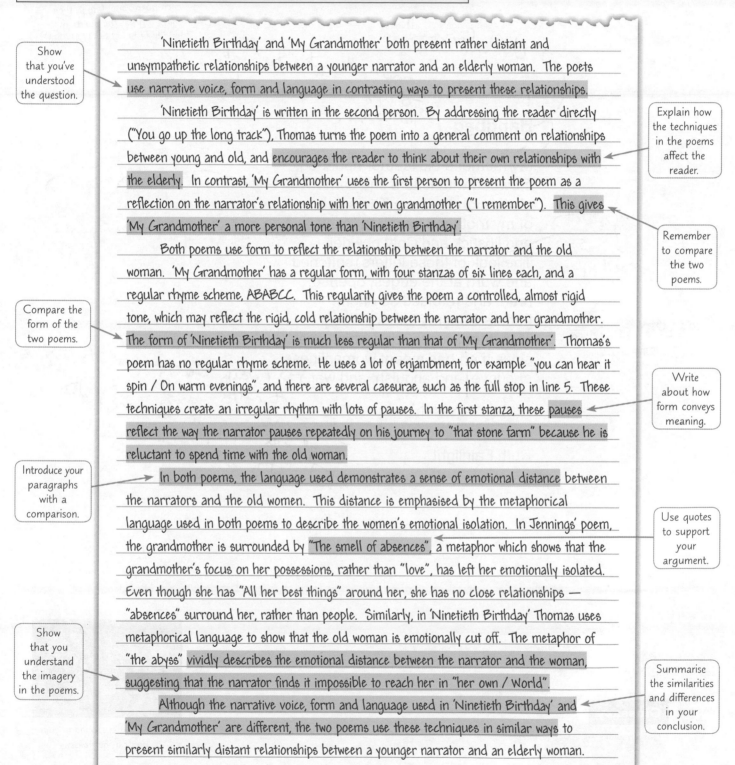

Show that you've understood the question.

'Ninetieth Birthday' and 'My Grandmother' both present rather distant and unsympathetic relationships between a younger narrator and an elderly woman. The poets use narrative voice, form and language in contrasting ways to present these relationships.

'Ninetieth Birthday' is written in the second person. By addressing the reader directly ("You go up the long track"), Thomas turns the poem into a general comment on relationships between young and old, and encourages the reader to think about their own relationships with the elderly. In contrast, 'My Grandmother' uses the first person to present the poem as a reflection on the narrator's relationship with her own grandmother ("I remember"). This gives 'My Grandmother' a more personal tone than 'Ninetieth Birthday'.

Explain how the techniques in the poems affect the reader.

Remember to compare the two poems.

Compare the form of the two poems.

Both poems use form to reflect the relationship between the narrator and the old woman. 'My Grandmother' has a regular form, with four stanzas of six lines each, and a regular rhyme scheme, ABABCC. This regularity gives the poem a controlled, almost rigid tone, which may reflect the rigid, cold relationship between the narrator and her grandmother. The form of 'Ninetieth Birthday' is much less regular than that of 'My Grandmother'. Thomas's poem has no regular rhyme scheme. He uses a lot of enjambment, for example "you can hear it spin / On warm evenings", and there are several caesurae, such as the full stop in line 5. These techniques create an irregular rhythm with lots of pauses. In the first stanza, these pauses reflect the way the narrator pauses repeatedly on his journey to "that stone farm" because he is reluctant to spend time with the old woman.

Write about how form conveys meaning.

Introduce your paragraphs with a comparison.

In both poems, the language used demonstrates a sense of emotional distance between the narrators and the old women. This distance is emphasised by the metaphorical language used in both poems to describe the women's emotional isolation. In Jennings' poem, the grandmother is surrounded by "The smell of absences", a metaphor which shows that the grandmother's focus on her possessions, rather than "love", has left her emotionally isolated. Even though she has "All her best things" around her, she has no close relationships — "absences" surround her, rather than people. Similarly, in 'Ninetieth Birthday' Thomas uses metaphorical language to show that the old woman is emotionally cut off. The metaphor of "the abyss" vividly describes the emotional distance between the narrator and the woman, suggesting that the narrator finds it impossible to reach her in "her own / World".

Use quotes to support your argument.

Show that you understand the imagery in the poems.

Although the narrative voice, form and language used in 'Ninetieth Birthday' and 'My Grandmother' are different, the two poems use these techniques in similar ways to present similarly distant relationships between a younger narrator and an elderly woman.

Summarise the similarities and differences in your conclusion.

Think about how to organise your time in the exam...

There's lots to do in Paper 2, so you need to keep an eye on the clock. Think about how many marks you can get for each question, and make sure you spend more time on the questions that are worth the most marks.

Handbag

Ruth Fainlight was born in New York in 1931, but moved to England when she was fifteen. She's published **short stories** and **poems**, including this one about her mum's old handbag.

[Handwritten annotations:]
Title: Personal.
Possessive pronoun depicts the speaker's love for her mother, creating a sense of nostalgia.

Handbag

My mother's old leather handbag,
crowded with letters she carried *[→ Enjambment heightens experience]*
all through the war. The smell
of my mother's handbag: mints *[→ Known smells suggest recent passing]*
5 and lipstick and Coty powder.
The look of those letters, softened
and worn at the edges, opened,
read, and refolded so often.
Letters from my father. Odour
10 of leather and powder, which ever
since then has meant womanliness,
and love, and anguish, and war.

[Annotations:] Alliteration / Vivid appearance / Letters are important. / Gunshots? / Listing → represents this one mother that the speaker will never see again. / I stanza conveys the tone's...

Ruth Fainlight

Carrying letters round in your bag can get messy.

Glossary

Coty powder — a face powder

Ruth Fainlight

I know by now you'll be desperate to show off your **poetry analysis skills**, so here's your chance...
Read and **annotate** the poem on page 14, then have a go at answering these **questions**.

Warm-up Questions

1) Explain briefly what you think the poem is about.

   A narrator looking through their mum's handbag.

2) Why do you think the narrator is looking through her mother's bag now?

   Perhaps the mother has died and it's a way of the speaker remembering her.

3) What does the phrase "crowded with letters" suggest about the narrator's mother?

   Suggests loneliness as the handbag was full of paper, not memories of others.

4) The poet repeats the word "and" three times in the final line. What effect does this have?

   Slows the pace of the poem.

5) Why do you think "Letters from my father." is the only complete sentence written on a single line?

   Highlights the importance of those specific letters.

6) How does the poet use the sense of touch in this poem?

   To show how valuable the mother's husband's letters were and that they were handled with care.

7) Find an example of enjambment in the poem and explain its effect.

   "carried / all through war" → Shows war's impact and expresses importance of letters.

8) What do you notice about the rhythm of the poem? What effect does this have?

   No regular rhyme scheme or particular rhythm, subtly creating a rather melancholic tone.

9) Find an example of alliteration in the poem. What effect does it have?

   "look of the letters" → emphasises the appearance and hint that they were looked at frequently.

Focus on... Mood

The mood of the poem is the general atmosphere that the poet creates for the reader.
Language, form and structure can all help create the mood of the poem.

1) a) Briefly describe the mood of the poem. *Loving, memorable mood that's also sombre and melancholic*

   b) How does the poet create this mood? *The poet shows the mother's love for her husband, creating nostalgia, but as we know they're both dead it makes the nostalgia melancholic.*

2) What effect does the sense of smell have on the mood of the poem?

   Smells depict fond and vivid memories that the mother went through and experienced.

3) How does the viewpoint used in this poem help create the mood?

   1st person creates a personal, emotional connection w/ the speaker and we feel her grief.

Exam-style Question — Part 1

What do you think the narrator is saying about her mother? How are these ideas presented?

Part 2 of the exam question will ask you to compare two poems. When you've finished answering Part 1, turn over for the next poem and Part 2.

Section Two — Unseen Poetry Practice

Jumper

Tony Harrison was born in Leeds in 1937. He has written **plays** and **poetry**, as well as **translating** works from ancient Greek and French. This poem was published in the **1970s**, but part of it is a memory from **World War Two**. During the war, people hid in bomb shelters for **protection** during bombing raids.

Jumper

When I want some sort of human metronome
to beat calm celebration out of fear
like that when German bombs fell round our home
it's my mother's needles, knitting, that I hear,
5   the click of needles steady though walls shake.
The stitches, plain or purl, were never dropped.
Bombs fell all that night until daybreak
but, not for a moment, did the knitting stop.
Though we shivered in the cellar-shelter's cold
10   and the whistling bombs sent shivers through the walls
I know now why she made her scared child hold
the skeins she wound so calmly into balls.

We open presents wrapped before she died.
With that same composure shown in that attack
15   she'd known the time to lay her wools aside —

the jumper I open's shop-bought, and is black!

Tony Harrison

Glossary

metronome — a machine that ticks at a constant speed to help musicians stay in time
plain and purl — types of stitch in knitting
skein — a length of wool that has been loosely twisted or coiled

Tony Harrison

In the exam you'll have to read not one but **two poems**, and the second question will ask you to **compare** them. Have a go at these **questions** to help you get to grips with 'Jumper', then try the exam-style question.

Warm-up Questions

1) Explain briefly what you think the poem is about.

2) How does the poet suggest that he and his mother were in danger during the bombing?

3) Why do you think the narrator's mother made him hold the wool as she was knitting?

4) Briefly describe the emotions that the poet puts across. How does the poet show these emotions?

5) The poet uses the words "shivered" and "shivers" on consecutive lines. What effect does this have?

6) How does the poet use the senses in the poem? Do you think this is effective?

7) Find an example of onomatopoeia in the poem and explain its effect.

8) What do you notice about the rhythm of the poem? What effect does this have?

9) Why do you think it is significant that the jumper is "shop-bought" and "black"? Why has this description been separated from the rest of the stanza?

Focus on... Form

The form of a poem refers to the type of poem (e.g. a sonnet) and its features, such as the number of lines, rhyme scheme and rhythm. It can emphasise the mood of a poem, or reflect its key ideas.

1) a) Briefly describe the poem's rhyme scheme.
    b) What effect does this have?

2) a) How are the last four lines different from the first twelve lines?
    b) Why do you think the poet has done this?

Exam-style Question — Part 2

The narrators of 'Handbag' and 'Jumper' both use an object to convey their feelings about their mothers. What similarities and differences are there in the way these feelings are conveyed?

'I Look Into My Glass'

Thomas Hardy (1840-1928) originally trained as an **architect**, but decided to give it up to become a **poet** and **author**. He wrote around **twenty novels** and several **poetry collections**.

'I Look Into My Glass'

I look into my glass,
And view my wasting skin,
And say, 'Would God it came to pass
My heart had shrunk as thin!'

5   For then, I, undistrest
By hearts grown cold to me,
Could lonely wait my endless rest
With equanimity.

But Time, to make me grieve,
10   Part steals, lets part abide;
And shakes this fragile frame at eve
With throbbings of noontide.

Thomas Hardy

Glossary

glass — mirror
wasting — getting less healthy
undistrest — made-up word meaning 'not worried'
equanimity — calmness
abide — stay

Li finally got the mirror to give him
the reflection he wanted.

Thomas Hardy

Have a bash at these **warm-up questions** to help you get to grips with the poem. Once you feel like you know it inside out, you're ready to write a stunning answer to the **exam-style question**.

Warm-up Questions

1) In just one sentence, explain what you think the poem is about.

2) Describe the mood of the poem. How does the poet create this mood?

3) What does the sentence "Would God it came to pass / My heart had shrunk as thin!" mean?

4) Explain the meaning of the phrase "throbbings of noontide".

5) What does the 2nd stanza tell you about the narrator's attitude towards death?

6) How does the poet create a contrast between youth and old age in the final stanza?

7) What is the poem's rhyme scheme? What effect does it have?

8) How does the poet use personification in the final stanza of the poem? Why do you think he uses this technique?

9) Explain how the poet's use of punctuation affects the pace of the final stanza.

Focus on... Sound

Poems are often intended to be read aloud, so the sound of the words is particularly important. The poet might repeat similar sounds to create a particular mood or to add extra impact.

1) a) Find an example of alliteration in the poem.
   b) Explain the effect of this.

2) a) Find some examples of assonance in the 2nd stanza.
   b) What does the assonance suggest about the narrator's feelings towards growing old?

Exam-style Question — Part 1

How does the narrator feel about getting older? How does he present these feelings?

When You Are Old

W.B. (William Butler, in case you're wondering) Yeats (1865-1939) is one of Ireland's **best-known** poets. His poetry is so good that he even won a **Nobel Prize in Literature**. Impressive...

When You Are Old

When you are old and grey and full of sleep,
And nodding by the fire, take down this book,
And slowly read, and dream of the soft look
Your eyes had once, and of their shadows deep;

5   How many loved your moments of glad grace,
And loved your beauty with love false or true,
But one man loved the pilgrim soul in you,
And loved the sorrows of your changing face;

And bending down beside the glowing bars,
10   Murmur, a little sadly, how Love fled
And paced upon the mountains overhead
And hid his face amid a crowd of stars.

W. B. Yeats

W.B. Yeats

And here's the second set of **questions** for your delight and delectation. Remember to keep flicking back to 'I Look Into My Glass' on p.18 as you answer the **exam-style question**, to make sure you haven't missed anything.

Warm-up Questions

1) Who do you think the narrator is addressing?

2) Briefly describe what you think the poem is about.

3) Describe the mood of the 1st stanza. How does the poet create this mood?

4) How is the pace of the 1st stanza different to the pace of the 2nd? Why do you think they are different?

5) What is the poem's rhyme scheme? What effect does it have?

6) What do you think the "glowing bars" in line 9 represent?

7) According to the narrator, how will the subject feel in old age? How are these feelings put across?

8) Find an example of personification in the poem and explain its effect.

9) Comment on the rhythm of the poem. What effect does this have on the reader?

Focus on... Repetition

Repetition can have a variety of different effects — for example, it could be used to emphasise important ideas in the poem or to create a strong sense of rhythm.

1) The poet repeats the word "and" six times in the 1st stanza. Why do you think he does this?

2) a) Which word is repeated in every line of the 2nd stanza?

   b) What is the effect of this repetition?

Exam-style Question — Part 2

The narrators of 'I Look Into My Glass' and 'When You Are Old' both consider the effects of ageing. What similarities and differences are there in the way these effects are presented?

The Dead-Beat

Wilfred Owen wrote this poem during the **First World War**, so don't go expecting it to be full of **rainbows** and **rays of sunshine**. I'll warn you, it's pretty **bleak**, but it's definitely worth a read...

The Dead-Beat

He dropped, — more sullenly than wearily,
Lay stupid like a cod, heavy like meat,
And none of us could kick him to his feet;
— Just blinked at my revolver, blearily;
5   — Didn't appear to know a war was on,
Or see the blasted trench at which he stared.
'I'll do 'em in,' he whined. 'If this hand's spared,
I'll murder them, I will.'
                                          A low voice said,
10   'It's Blighty, p'raps, he sees; his pluck's all gone,
Dreaming of all the valiant, that *aren't* dead:
Bold uncles, smiling ministerially;
Maybe his brave young wife, getting her fun
In some new home, improved materially.
15   It's not these stiffs have crazed him; nor the Hun.'

We sent him down at last, out of the way.
Unwounded; — stout lad, too, before that strafe.
Malingering? Stretcher-bearers winked, 'Not half!'

Next day I heard the Doc's well-whiskied laugh:
20   'That scum you sent last night soon died. Hooray!'

Wilfred Owen

Glossary

Blighty — a nickname for Britain
pluck — courage
ministerially — like a church minister
stiffs — dead bodies
Hun — a nickname for German soldiers (the enemy)
strafe — an attack by low-flying aircraft
malingering — to fake or exaggerate an illness to get out of something

Wilfred Owen

I'm sure you're eager for **more** questions by now, and it's your lucky day... Here are some questions about the poem on page 22 — have a good **read** of the poem before you **answer** them.

Warm-up Questions

1) Write down what you think the poem is about, in just one sentence.

2) Why do you think the poet compares the man to "a cod" and "meat"?

3) People try to "kick him to his feet". What does the word "kick" suggest about life in the trenches?

4) Why do you think the poet describes people at home as "valiant", "Bold" and "brave"?

5) How do the medical staff react to the patient? What do you think about their reactions?

6) What do you think of the title of this poem? Why do you think the poet chose this title?

7) What do you notice about the rhyme scheme of the poem? What effect does this have?

8) Wilfred Owen felt sympathy for soldiers who had breakdowns during the war.
   How does the attitude of the narrator differ from this view?

Focus on... Voice

The voice of the poem refers to the person narrating the poem — it may be the poet themselves or a character they've created. The speaker's vocabulary and how they speak can hint at their character.

1) The poet uses direct speech in this poem. What effect does this have on the reader?

2) a) Find three examples of colloquial language in the poem.

   b) Why do you think the poet uses elements of colloquial language in the poem?

3) The poem ends with the word "Hooray!" What effect does this have?

Exam-style Question — Part 1

What is the poet saying about how war changes people's behaviour, and how does he convey this to the reader?

Spring in War-Time

Edith Nesbit (1858-1924) is famous for writing a book called **The Railway Children**, but she wrote many volumes of poetry too. She was also very interested in **politics**, but I'm not sure that shows in this poem...

Spring in War-Time

Now the sprinkled blackthorn snow
Lies along the lovers' lane
Where last year we used to go—
Where we shall not go again.

5   In the hedge the buds are new,
By our wood the violets peer—
Just like last year's violets, too,
But they have no scent this year.

Every bird has heart to sing
10   Of its nest, warmed by its breast;
We had heart to sing last spring,
But we never built our nest.

Presently red roses blown
Will make all the garden gay...
15   Not yet have the daisies grown
On your clay.

Edith Nesbit

Glossary

blackthorn — a bush with white flowers in spring

Edith Nesbit

Before you answer these questions, **read** the poem all the way through **slowly**. Read it again and **underline** the bits that stand out to you. Then, and only then, are you ready to answer the questions, grasshopper.

Warm-up Questions

1) Write down what you think the poem is about, in just one sentence.

2) Who do you think the narrator is addressing in this poem?

3) What do you think the narrator means by "we never built our nest" in the 3rd stanza?

4) What do you think the narrator means when she says that the violets "have no scent this year"?

5) How does the poet link daisies and death in the last stanza?

6) What is the rhyme scheme of this poem and why do you think that the poet chose it?

7) The last line of the poem has a different rhythm. Why do you think that the poet has done this?

8) Which of the four stanzas do you find the most effective in showing the narrator's emotions? Give a reason for your answer.

Focus on... Contrasts

Contrasts can emphasise differences or create a sense of balance in a poem. Juxtaposition highlights differences by putting two ideas close to each other to encourage the reader to contrast them.

1) What does the poet contrast with the narrator's feelings in the poem?

2) How does the poet use the poem's structure to highlight the contrast you chose in question one?

3) What is the effect of the contrast you chose in question one on the reader?

Exam-style Question — Part 2

Both 'The Dead-Beat' and 'Spring in War-Time' consider the effects of war. What similarities and differences are there in the methods used to present these effects?

The Bereavement of the Lion-Keeper

Sheenagh Pugh is a British **poet**, **novelist** and **translator**. She lives in Shetland, and lots of her poems feature northern European landscapes. Not this one though — this one's about lions...

The Bereavement of the Lion-Keeper

for Sheraq Omar

Who stayed, long after his pay stopped,
in the zoo with no visitors,
just keepers and captives, moth-eaten,
growing old together.

5   Who begged for meat in the market-place
as times grew hungrier,
and cut it up small to feed him,
since his teeth were gone.

Who could stroke his head, who knew
10   how it felt to plunge fingers
into rough glowing fur, who has heard
the deepest purr in the world.

Who curled close to him, wrapped in his warmth,
his pungent scent, as the bombs fell,
15   who has seen him asleep so often,
but never like this.

Who knew that elderly lions
were not immortal, that it was bound
to happen, that he died peacefully,
20   in the course of nature,

but who knows no way to let go
of love, to walk out of sunlight,
to be an old man in a city
without a lion.

This poem is about Marjan, a lion who lived in Kabul Zoo in Afghanistan for 23 years until his death in 2002. Sheraq Omar, whom the poem is dedicated to, was Marjan's keeper.

Sheenagh Pugh

Sheenagh Pugh

Sob This is such a sad poem. I'm going in search of cake and ice cream to cheer myself up. You, however, need to have a go at these **questions** before you indulge in any sugary treats. Sorry about that.

Warm-up Questions

1) Briefly describe what you think the poem is about.

2) How does the poet suggest that the keepers were devoted to the animals and their jobs?

3) Each stanza apart from the last one starts with the word "Who...". What is the effect of this?

4) What does "who has seen him asleep so often, / but never like this." mean?

5) What do you think the line "wrapped in his warmth, / his pungent scent, as the bombs fell," suggests?

6) How does the poet appeal to different senses? Give some examples and explain their effect.

7) a) In what way does the poem show similarities between the ageing lion and the elderly keeper?
   b) How does that make the reader feel?

8) Do you think there is a feeling of hope in the poem? Pick out some quotes to explain your view.

9) Which of the six stanzas do you find the most effective in showing the keeper's emotions? Explain your answer.

Focus on... Tone

The tone of the poem is the mood or feeling suggested by the way the poet writes.
The poet's choice of language and the voice the poem is written in can help create the poem's tone.

1) a) Briefly describe the overall tone of the poem.
   b) What language does the poet use to create this tone?

2) How does the tone of the poem change in the final stanza?

Exam-style Question — Part 1

What does the poem say about man's relationship with animals?
How does the poet put these ideas across?

The Tyger

This poem was published in **1794**, so it's pretty **old**. Blake **illustrated** the original version of the poem himself — he drew a big picture of a **tiger** at the bottom. Lovely.

The Tyger

Tyger! Tyger! burning bright
In the forests of the night,
What immortal hand or eye
Could frame thy fearful symmetry?

5   In what distant deeps or skies
Burnt the fire of thine eyes?
On what wings dare he aspire?
What the hand dare seize the fire?

And what shoulder, and what art,
10   Could twist the sinews of thy heart?
And when thy heart began to beat,
What dread hand? and what dread feet?

What the hammer? what the chain?
In what furnace was thy brain?
15   What the anvil? what dread grasp
Dare its deadly terrors clasp?

When the stars threw down their spears,
And water'd heaven with their tears,
Did he smile his work to see?
20   Did he who made the Lamb make thee?

Tyger! Tyger! burning bright
In the forests of the night,
What immortal hand or eye,
Dare frame thy fearful symmetry?

William Blake

Will's pet cat was starting to get annoyed at the constant questions.

Glossary

frame — design or create
aspire — to strive towards an achievement
sinews — tendons or muscles
dread — frightening and awe-inspiring

William Blake

Your next mission, should you choose to accept it, is to have a good **read** of the poem on page 28, **annotate** the most important bits, then have a go at **answering** these questions.

Warm-up Questions

1) Briefly explain what you think the poem is about.

2) What attitude do you think the narrator has towards the tiger?

3) Give one example of a contrast in the poem. What effect does this have?

4) Why do you think the poet only mentions some parts of the tiger's creator, like the "hand" and "eye"?

5) The poem is made up almost entirely of questions. What effect does this have?

6) Give one example of alliteration in the poem. What does the alliteration achieve?

7) Comment on the rhythm of the poem. What effect does this have on the reader?

8) Why does the poet ask "Did he who made the Lamb make thee?"

9) a) Why does the poet repeat the first stanza at the end of the poem?
   b) Why does he replace the word "Could" with "Dare"?

Focus on... Imagery

Imagery is language that creates a picture in your mind — for example, personification, metaphors or similes. Poets use imagery to create powerful descriptions or to achieve a certain effect on the reader.

1) a) Find one example of fire imagery in the poem.

   b) What effect does this have?

2) a) Give one example of personification in the poem.

   b) What is the effect of this?

3) Which of the images in the poem do you think is the most effective? Explain your answer.

Exam-style Question — Part 2

Compare the methods the poets use to present attitudes towards animals in 'The Bereavement of the Lion-Keeper' and 'The Tyger'.

A century later

This poem is about **Malala Yousafzai**, a Pakistani schoolgirl who **survived** being **shot** in the head for speaking out about **girls'** right to **education**. Malala went on to win the 2014 **Nobel Peace Prize** for her actions.

A century later

The school-bell is a call to battle,
every step to class, a step into the firing-line.
Here is the target, fine skin at the temple,
cheek still rounded from being fifteen.

5   Surrendered, surrounded, she
takes the bullet in the head

and walks on. The missile cuts
a pathway in her mind, to an orchard
in full bloom, a field humming under the sun,
10   its lap open and full of poppies.

This girl has won
the right to be ordinary,

wear bangles to a wedding, paint her fingernails,
go to school. *Bullet*, she says, *you are stupid.*
15   *You have failed. You cannot kill a book*
or the buzzing in it.

A murmur, a swarm. Behind her, one by one,
the schoolgirls are standing up
to take their places on the front line.

Imtiaz Dharker

> This poem was written as a response to a poem by Wilfred Owen about young soldiers killed in World War One — hence the title 'A century later'.

Imtiaz Dharker

Once you feel like you know the **poem** on page 30 better than you know the way to the fridge, have a go at answering these **questions**. Don't forget to make a **plan** before you answer the exam-style question.

Warm-up Questions

1) Explain briefly what you think the poem is about.

2) What metaphor does the poet use to describe female education? What is the effect of this?

3) Why do you think the narrator describes the schoolgirl's cheek as "still rounded from being fifteen"?

4) In the 5th stanza, the poet includes the voice of the girl who was shot. What is the effect of this?

5) a) Briefly describe the mood of the poem.
   b) How does the poet create this mood?

6) Give one example of sibilance in the poem. What effect does the sibilance have?

7) a) What imagery does the poet use to describe the girl's experience of being shot?
   b) Why do you think the poet uses this description?

8) Give one example of personification in the poem. What effect does it have?

Focus on... Punctuation

Punctuation can alter the pace of the poem. Caesurae and end-stopping can create pauses in a poem, while enjambment can help the lines to flow and increase the pace.

1) Explain the effect of the punctuation used when the poet describes the girl being shot.

2) a) How is the girl's speech punctuated?
   b) What is the effect of this?

3) The final two lines of the poem use enjambment. What effect does this have?

Exam-style Question — Part 1

What does the poem suggest about the fight for female education? How does the poet present these ideas?

History Lesson

Natasha Trethewey is an **American poet**. Her poetry often focuses on the legacy of **racial inequality** in the United States — which might give you a clue about what's happening in this poem...

History Lesson

I am four in this photograph, standing
on a wide strip of Mississippi beach,
my hands on the flowered hips

of a bright bikini. My toes dig in,
5   curl around wet sand. The sun cuts
the rippling Gulf in flashes with each

tidal rush. Minnows dart at my feet
glinting like switchblades. I am alone
except for my grandmother, other side

10   of the camera, telling me how to pose.
It is 1970, two years after they opened
the rest of this beach to us,

forty years since the photograph
where she stood on a narrow plot
15   of sand marked *colored*, smiling,

her hands on the flowered hips
of a cotton meal-sack dress.

Natasha Trethewey

Glossary

Mississippi — a state in the south-east of the United States
Gulf — the coastline of the south-eastern USA
minnows — small fish that swim in large groups
switchblades — knives with a folding blade hidden in the handle which are widely illegal
meal-sack dress — a dress made from sacks, which was often worn by poorer women
                in rural areas of the US in the late 19th and early 20th centuries

Natasha Trethewey

Woo — this is it, your final set of **practice questions**. When you've finished these, you should be able to analyse poetry with the best of 'em, which will put you in prime position for the exam...

Warm-up Questions

1) In just one sentence, write down what you think the poem is about.

2) Find an example of enjambment in the poem and explain its effect.

3) Why do you think the poet chose the title 'History Lesson'? Do you think it is an effective title?

4) Find one example of a simile in the poem. What is the effect of this?

5) Give one similarity and one difference between the photograph of the narrator in 1970 and the photograph of her grandmother 40 years earlier.

6) What do lines 11-12 suggest about the narrator's life?

7) Find one example of alliteration in the poem. What effect does it have?

8) How does the poet appeal to the sense of touch? Give an example and explain its effect.

9) Do you think the narrator admires her grandmother? Explain your answer.

Focus on... Structure

Structure refers to how the ideas progress through the poem — e.g. how it begins, develops and ends. The poem's structure can shape its meaning and emphasise important ideas or contrasts in the poem.

1) Briefly describe the poem's structure.

2) What is the effect of the poem's beginning?

3) The poem describes two photographs from different time periods. How does its structure:
   a) emphasise the similarities between the two time periods?
   b) emphasise the differences between the two time periods?

Exam-style Question — Part 2

The narrators of 'A century later' and 'History Lesson' both describe people overcoming inequalities in society. What similarities and differences are there in the way their ideas are conveyed?

Mark Scheme

I bet you've always wanted to be an **examiner** for the day, haven't you? Thought so. That's why I've given you **a whole section** where you can **mark** some **sample exam answers**. I knew you'd be pleased. But before you dive in, have a good look at these **mark schemes**...

This section lets you mark some sample answer extracts

1) **Marking extracts** from sample exam answers is a **great way** to find out **exactly** what you'll need to do to get the grade you want.

2) Remember, in this section you're only marking **extracts**, not full answers. The essays you'll write in the exam will be **longer** than the answer extracts on the next few pages.

3) The **mark schemes** on these two pages are similar to the ones your **examiner** will use. The idea is for **you** to use them to help you mark the sample answer extracts in the rest of the section.

4) These extracts should give you a good idea of what the examiner will be looking for when he or she marks **your exam answer**. Don't forget, **grade 9** is the **top grade** you can get in the exam.

5) So before you do anything else, **read the mark schemes** and make sure you **understand** them.

Use this mark scheme to mark the answers to Question 1

Grade	Assessment Objective	What you've written
8-9	**AO1**	• Shows a critical, convincing and well-structured analysis of the poem • Uses well-chosen examples to support interpretation(s)
	AO2	• Gives an insightful analysis of the poet's use of language, structure and form, using technical terms effectively • Presents a detailed exploration of how the poet's techniques affect the reader
6-7	**AO1**	• Presents a thoughtful, well-developed analysis of the poem • Uses a range of examples to support the interpretation(s)
	AO2	• Explores the poet's use of language and/or structure and/or form in detail, using correct technical terms • Examines the effect of the poet's techniques on the reader
4-5	**AO1**	• Gives a clear analysis of the poem • Provides some references and detail related to interpretation of the poem
	AO2	• Gives some explanation of the poet's use of language and/or structure and/or form, using some relevant technical terms • Explains how some of the techniques used in the poem affect the reader

You can also be awarded **grades 1-3**. We **haven't included** any **sample answer extracts** at 1-3 level though — so those grades aren't in this mark scheme.

Mark Scheme

Here's another lovely **mark scheme** for you — this one should give you a **good idea** of the sort of thing you need to do in **your answer** to Question 2. Remember, **Question 2** will ask you to write about **two** poems...

Use this mark scheme to mark the answers to Question 2

1) Question 2 will ask you to **compare** two poems.

2) Remember, this question is **only** worth **8 marks**, so you **don't** want to spend **too long** on your answer.

3) This question is all about the **techniques** the poets have used and how they **affect the reader**. Your answer must focus on **similarities** and **differences** between the **language**, **form** and **structure** used in the two poems.

Grade	Assessment Objective	What you've written
8-9	AO2	• Explores similarities and differences between the use of language, structure and form in the two poems, using technical terms effectively • Convincingly explores and compares the ways the poets' techniques affect the reader
6-7	AO2	• Gives a thoughtful comparison of the poets' use of language and/or structure and/or form, using appropriate technical terms • Compares the effects of the poets' techniques on the reader
4-5	AO2	• Compares how the poets have used language and/or structure and/or form, using some relevant technical terms • Compares the way some of the poets' techniques affect the reader

You can also be awarded **grades 1-3**. We **haven't included** any **sample answer extracts** at 1-3 level though — so those grades aren't in this mark scheme.

Look out for quotes and examples in the answer extracts

1) When the examiner marks your answers, they will be paying close attention to whether you've used quotes and examples from the poems to back up your arguments.

2) Think like an examiner when you're marking the answer extracts on the next few pages and look out for the way they use evidence from the poems:

You can find more about how to write a good answer on pages 3-7.

- The quotes and examples should have been carefully chosen — they must be relevant to the point being made.

- There's no need to quote large chunks of text.

- Exact quotes should be inside quotation marks (" ") like this: "I believe life ends with death."

- If the text has been rephrased, you don't need quotation marks.

  E.g. The poet believes that life does not go on beyond death.

- Wherever possible, quotes should be integrated into the sentences so that the writing flows nicely.

  E.g. The blunt, "I believe life ends with death", makes the narrator sound cold and definite.

Composed Upon Westminster Bridge

William Wordsworth (1770-1850) was one of the most famous of the **Romantic poets**. His best-known poem is 'I Wandered Lonely as a Cloud' which, like many of his poems, is about the beauty of **nature**.

> Q1   Read the poem below. What are the narrator's feelings about the city?
> What methods does the poet use to put these emotions across?
>
> **(24 marks)**

Composed Upon Westminster Bridge, Sept. 3, 1802

Earth has not anything to show more fair:
Dull would he be of soul who could pass by
A sight so touching in its majesty:
This City now doth, like a garment, wear
5   The beauty of the morning; silent, bare,
Ships, towers, domes, theatres, and temples lie
Open unto the fields, and to the sky;
All bright and glittering in the smokeless air.
Never did sun more beautifully steep
10   In his first splendour, valley, rock, or hill;
Ne'er saw I, never felt, a calm so deep!
The river glideth at his own sweet will:
Dear God! the very houses seem asleep;
And all that mighty heart is lying still!

William Wordsworth

Ahh, beauteous London.

William Wordsworth

Here's your first set of **sample answer extracts**. For each one, think about where it fits in the **mark scheme** for **Question 1** on **p.36**. Most answers won't fit the criteria for one band exactly — it's about finding the **best fit**.

1

> The narrator thinks the city is really amazing and impressive. The poet shows this right at the start with the opening line, "Earth has not anything to show more fair". The narrator thinks the city is the most beautiful thing in the world, which is a bit over-the-top, and makes him sound really impressed and amazed. The line "Ne'er saw I, never felt, a calm so deep!" shows how amazed the narrator is too, especially the exclamation mark. The narrator also says "Dear God!" in line 13. That's the sort of thing you say when you're excited about something, so it shows that the narrator's excited about the city and thinks it's amazing.

a) Write down the grade band (4-5, 6-7 or 8-9) that you think this answer falls into.

b) Give at least two reasons why you chose that grade.

2

> Using hyperbole, the narrator claims that there is nothing in the world "more fair" than the sight of London at dawn. The narrator is so awestruck by the city's beauty that he almost seems to be in love with it. Wordsworth's personification of the city as wearing "The beauty of the morning" makes the city sound elegant and graceful, creating an image of it as a beautiful woman, whom the narrator lovingly admires.
>
> The poem is written as a Petrarchan sonnet, and this also suggests the narrator's love for the city. This form is usually used for love poetry, so Wordsworth's choice of it to write about London reinforces the picture in the reader's mind of the city as a woman the narrator is in love with.

a) Write down the grade band (4-5, 6-7 or 8-9) that you think this answer falls into.

b) Give at least two reasons why you chose that grade.

3

> Wordsworth uses evocative imagery to show that the narrator finds London very beautiful. The phrase "bright and glittering" creates a beautiful image of sunlight shining on the city's buildings, suggesting the way precious jewels catch the light. The use of personification — "This City now doth, like a garment, wear / The beauty of the morning" — also emphasises London's beauty, making it sound elegant and graceful.
>
> Wordsworth also uses hyperbole to show how beautiful the narrator finds the city. For example, the phrase "Never did sun more beautifully steep / In his first splendour, valley, rock, or hill" describes the sunrise over the city as more beautiful than any the narrator has seen in the countryside. This exaggerated claim makes the narrator seem amazed and awestruck by the city's appearance.

a) Write down the grade band (4-5, 6-7 or 8-9) that you think this answer falls into.

b) Give at least two reasons why you chose that grade.

London

Claude McKay (1889-1948) was a Jamaican poet and writer. He was a key figure in the Harlem Renaissance, an African-American cultural movement in the United States from the 1910s to the 1930s.

> Q2 Read the poem below. In both 'Composed upon Westminster Bridge' and 'London', the poets describe London.
> What are the similarities and differences in the methods the poets use to describe London?
>
> **(8 marks)**

London

The fog prevails above all in my mind,
Wrapping around me like a cold grey sheet,
And shutting out the city, which oppressed
My spirit even like Teutonic art in stone.
5   A city without light and without heat,
Whose colour was like iron in my breast
And freezing through my body to the bone:
Oh blessed was the fog that veiled me blind!

But how could I, tropical African,
10   Who claim the sun as my authentic sire,
Find beauty in that chilling atmosphere?
Ancestral intellect could help me bear
A little while, but surely not admire
The civilisation of the Englishman.

Claude McKay

Ruby preferred her tartan
blanket to a cold grey sheet.

Glossary

Teutonic — an old word meaning 'relating to people of German origin'
sire — father

Section Three — Marking Sample Answers

Claude McKay

Question 2 asks you to **compare** two poems, so here you're looking for answers that discuss **similarities** and **differences** between the poems. You'll need the mark scheme on **page 35** for these answers extracts...

1

The two poems depict London's atmosphere very differently. In Wordsworth's poem, London is "calm" and "asleep" in "The beauty of the morning", whereas McKay's London is "without light and without heat" and has a "chilling atmosphere". Both poets use rhyme to create the atmosphere they describe. Wordsworth's poem is written in the form of a Petrarchan sonnet, so it has the rhyme scheme ABBA, ABBA, CDCDCD. The regularity of this rhyme scheme gives the poem a tranquil atmosphere, which mirrors the "deep" calm in the "silent" city. In contrast, 'London' has an unusual rhyme scheme, ABCDBCDA, EFGGFE, in which the first and last lines of each stanza rhyme. In the first stanza, this rhyme closely links "mind" and "blind", emphasising the smothering effect of the fog that obstructs the narrator's sight. These rhymes contribute to the cold, dark atmosphere in the poem, which reflects the sense of oppression experienced by the narrator in the city.

a)   Write down the grade band (4-5, 6-7 or 8-9) that you think this answer falls into.
b)   Give at least two reasons why you chose that grade.

2

Wordsworth and McKay both use figurative language to vividly describe London. Wordsworth says that London is wearing the "beauty of the morning" "like a garment", and describes the city using the metaphor of a "mighty heart". He also personifies the Thames — it "glideth at his own sweet will". This suggests that the city is alive and has a "will" of its own, independent from the people who live in it. In contrast, McKay uses a simile to describe how the city fog wraps around the narrator "like a cold grey sheet" and uses another simile to describe how London's "colour was like iron". Unlike Wordsworth's poem, this metallic colour gives the reader an impression of a dull and lifeless city.

a)   Write down the grade band (4-5, 6-7 or 8-9) that you think this answer falls into.
b)   Give at least two reasons why you chose that grade.

3

Both poems describe the cities through similes. In 'Composed Upon Westminster Bridge, Sept. 3, 1802', the poet says "This City now doth, like a garment, wear / The beauty of the morning". This sounds really pretty and gives you a good picture of what the city looks like in the early morning. In 'London', the poet also describes the city through similes. For example, he says the city's colour is "like iron in my breast", and this helps you imagine how grey and gloomy the city looks when it's foggy.

a)   Write down the grade band (4-5, 6-7 or 8-9) that you think this answer falls into.
b)   Give at least two reasons why you chose that grade.

Eating Poetry

Mark Strand was born in Canada but grew up in North, Central and South America. He served as the US **Poet Laureate** and was awarded the **Pulitzer Prize for Poetry** in 1999 for his poetry collection *Blizzard of One*.

> Q1   Read the poem below. What do you think the poet is saying
> about imagination and reality? How does he present these ideas?
>
> **(24 marks)**

Eating Poetry

Ink runs from the corners of my mouth.
There is no happiness like mine.
I have been eating poetry.

The librarian does not believe what she sees.
5   Her eyes are sad
and she walks with her hands in her dress.

The poems are gone.
The light is dim.
The dogs are on the basement stairs and coming up.

10   Their eyeballs roll,
their blond legs burn like brush.
The poor librarian begins to stamp her feet and weep.

She does not understand.
When I get on my knees and lick her hand,
15   she screams.

I am a new man.
I snarl at her and bark.
I romp with joy in the bookish dark.

Mark Strand

Emily thought that eating
pottery was a great idea.

Mark Strand

Here are some more sample answers extracts, so have another try at giving them a grade.
Don't forget to explain what's wrong with the answer as well as what's right.

1

　　　　The narrator hasn't really been "eating poetry", it's just a metaphor. He's actually been reading poetry, and it makes him really happy — "There is no happiness like mine". The line "I romp with joy in the bookish dark" also shows you that reading makes the narrator really happy. Not everyone is happy though. The librarian is "sad" and she seems angry with the narrator. She "begins to stamp her feet" and "she screams". This shows that even if imagination makes you really happy, some people won't like it if you get carried away with imagination, and instead they'll want you to be sensible all the time.

a)　　　Write down the grade band (4-5, 6-7 or 8-9) that you think this answer falls into.

b)　　　Give at least two reasons why you chose that grade.

2

　　　　The librarian may represent those outside the narrator's imaginary world. The use of the phrase "does not understand" in one of only two rhyming couplets in the poem shows how incomprehensible the librarian finds the narrator's behaviour. The poet uses assonant "ee" sounds to emphasise how angry and upset the librarian is — she "stamp[s] her feet and weep[s]". The librarian's response to the narrator shows that an individual's imaginary world can seem incomprehensible and even frightening to those outside it.

　　　　The poet describes the librarian using lots of sibilant 's' sounds, e.g. "sees", "sad" and "dress", which reflect the "sshh" she might say in a library. This suggests that the librarian represents those who control access to books. The contrast between the narrator's "happiness" and the librarian's "sad" eyes and fearful response to him ("she screams") suggests that, even though such figures spend their time surrounded by books, they may "not understand" the world of imagination that books can open up.

a)　　　Write down the grade band (4-5, 6-7 or 8-9) that you think this answer falls into.

b)　　　Give at least two reasons why you chose that grade.

3

　　　　The metaphor of "eating poetry" shows the "happiness" that comes from reading works of imagination. The image of "ink" running "from the corners" of the narrator's mouth vividly shows how much the narrator loves poetry, by likening it to something delicious that the narrator is really enjoying eating.

　　　　Although "eating poetry" makes the narrator happy, the imagery of the dogs suggests that the world of imagination might be dangerous. The sudden appearance of the dogs "on the basement stairs" is strange and a bit sinister and, combined with the alliterative description of their "blond legs", which "burn like brush", makes them sound almost devilish. The way the dogs' "eyeballs roll" makes them sound crazy, which reinforces the sense of danger that they pose.

a)　　　Write down the grade band (4-5, 6-7 or 8-9) that you think this answer falls into.

b)　　　Give at least two reasons why you chose that grade.

42

Volumes

Here's a poem that was published in **1992**. Fun Fact #35 — 1992 was **International Space Year**. It was also the 500th anniversary of **Columbus's** first voyage to America. Anyway, back to **poetry**...

> **Q2** Read the poem below. 'Eating Poetry' and 'Volumes' both present strong feelings about reading. What are the similarities and differences between the methods the poets use to put these feelings across?
>
> **(8 marks)**

Volumes

They put me in a fever. It's not enough
to look. I want to hold them all
and stuff them in the gaps in my head.
I gallop past Health towards Travel
5   where I break into a muck sweat
as I lift and sniff a book about Verona.
The odour makes me stagger and long
to be a book mite, to live right inside
and gulp holes through the picture maps.
10 I don't trust myself in Fiction. The thought
of those thousands and thousands of stories —
the crush and babble of other minds —
makes the whites of my eyes show and roll.
Last time I sauntered by those shelves
15 I slammed into the New Titles display
and crashed right through a pyramid of books
on to my back among the toppled photos
of authors winking at the carry on.
I got a cuppa and a pat on the rump
20 from the kind saleslady who has the bubble
of book hysteria herself, I'd guess.
If she could, she'd wear print on her skin.
There are words written for everything,
I think, and it's only a matter of time
25 before I find a new 'How To' book:
how to stand upright, how not to fall
and how not to cry out when you do.

Jo Shapcott

Jo Shapcott

You must be getting the **hang** of this now — if you get much more practice you'll be putting those English examiners out of a job. Remember, in these extracts you're looking for **comparison** of the two poems.

1

Both poems use form to represent the narrators' feelings about reading. 'Eating Poetry' is divided into short stanzas of just three lines. It uses short sentences and lots of end-stopped lines, and has no regular rhyme scheme. This gives the poem an uneven, stop-start rhythm, which creates the feeling that you are moving suddenly, almost at random, from one image to another, as you do in a dream. This dreamlike atmosphere represents the world of imagination that the narrator enters when he reads poetry. The form of 'Volumes' is very different, but it also reflects the way the narrator feels about reading. Like 'Eating Poetry', it has no regular rhyme scheme, but in contrast to Strand's poem, it is not divided into stanzas, and uses a lot of enjambment. This makes the poem seem chaotic and disorganised, mirroring the crazed "fever" the narrator experiences when she is surrounded by books.

a)   Write down the grade band (4-5, 6-7 or 8-9) that you think this answer falls into.

b)   Give at least two reasons why you chose that grade.

2

'Eating Poetry' and 'Volumes' both use animal imagery to convey the strength of the narrator's feelings about reading. In 'Eating Poetry', the narrator becomes dog-like: "I get on my knees and lick her hand", "I snarl at her and bark". In 'Volumes', meanwhile, the narrator "gallop[s]" and "break[s] into a muck sweat", which makes her sound like a horse. In both cases, this animal imagery suggests the narrators' overwhelming excitement about books and reading.

The narrator's dog-like behaviour in 'Eating Poetry' makes him seem unstable, as does the act of "eating poetry" itself. This suggests that love of reading is a sort of madness. Similarly, the narrator of 'Volumes' describes her love of books as "hysteria", a word usually linked to uncontrolled behaviour. She also says the thought of fiction makes the whites of her eyes "show and roll", which makes her sound erratic.

a)   Write down the grade band (4-5, 6-7 or 8-9) that you think this answer falls into.

b)   Give at least two reasons why you chose that grade.

3

Both poems describe eating books to show that the narrators love reading. The narrator of Strand's poem has been "eating poetry", and in 'Volumes' the narrator says she wants to "be a book mite" and "gulp holes" in the books. The narrators also behave like animals. For example, the narrator of 'Eating Poetry' says "I snarl at her and bark" like a dog, and the narrator of 'Volumes' says "I gallop" like a horse. This tells you how much of a strong effect reading has on the narrators. The narrator of 'Eating Poetry' sounds a bit unstable, and so does the narrator of 'Volumes' — she says books put her in a "fever" and she talks about "book hysteria". This shows that the narrators love reading so much it's made them unbalanced.

a)   Write down the grade band (4-5, 6-7 or 8-9) that you think this answer falls into.

b)   Give at least two reasons why you chose that grade.

Section Three — Marking Sample Answers

The Way Through the Woods

Rudyard Kipling (1865-1936) wrote **poetry**, **novels** and **short stories**. Fun fact #47: two lines of his most famous poem, '**If—**' are written on the wall above the players' entrance to Centre Court at Wimbledon.

> **Q1** Read the poem below. How does the poet present the way that the closed road has changed over time?
>
> **(24 marks)**

The Way Through the Woods

They shut the road through the woods
Seventy years ago.
Weather and rain have undone it again,
And now you would never know
5   There was once a road through the woods
Before they planted the trees.
It is underneath the coppice and heath,
And the thin anemones.
Only the keeper sees
10   That, where the ring-dove broods,
And the badgers roll at ease,
There was once a road through the woods.

Yet, if you enter the woods
Of a summer evening late,
15   When the night-air cools on the trout-ringed pools
Where the otter whistles his mate,
(They fear not men in the woods,
Because they see so few.)
You will hear the beat of a horse's feet,
20   And the swish of a skirt in the dew,
Steadily cantering through
The misty solitudes,
As though they perfectly knew
The old lost road through the woods...
25   But there is no road through the woods.

Rudyard Kipling

Glossary

anemone — a flower of the buttercup family

"I'm not brooding, actually. I'm thinking."

Rudyard Kipling

Have a gander at these sample answer extracts, then give them a grade. If in doubt, have a look back at the mark scheme on page 34 for a bit of guidance...

1

The way the road through the woods has changed over time is really mysterious. The road was shut a long time ago, and now it's really overgrown and it has pretty much disappeared. The poet says it's "underneath the coppice and heath" and "now you would never know" it was there, and this shows that the wood has grown over the road. There are still sounds of people using it though. For example, "You will hear the beat of a horse's feet" is a line that sounds like a horse riding along the road, and "the swish of a skirt" is onomatopoeic and makes you hear the sound of people who used to walk along the road. The fact you can hear people on the road even though it's gone makes you think they might be ghosts.

a)   Write down the grade band (4-5, 6-7 or 8-9) that you think this answer falls into.

b)   Give at least two reasons why you chose that grade.

2

The opening line of the poem, "They shut the road through the woods", uses single syllable words and heavy stresses on the words "shut", "road" and "woods" to make the closure of the road sound final and certain, and to give the impression that man is in control. However, the poem suggests that it is nature, rather than man, which has made the road disappear over time. For example, the use of internal rhyme makes the lines "Weather and rain has undone it again" and "It is underneath the coppice and heath" stand out, and this highlights the role that weather and plants have played in making the road disappear. Similarly, the image of "badgers roll[ing] at ease" suggests that animals have taken over the wood where the road used to be and made themselves at home there, while humans don't really go there any more.

a)   Write down the grade band (4-5, 6-7 or 8-9) that you think this answer falls into.

b)   Give at least two reasons why you chose that grade.

3

The poet suggests that, even though the road has been "undone" over time, so that now "you would never know" it was there, it has not disappeared entirely, but is still used by mysterious figures. These figures are described through sound, which makes them seem ghostly, as if they can be heard but not seen. For example, "You will hear the beat of a horse's feet" uses internal rhyme to mirror the sound of horses' hooves on the road, while "swish of a skirt" uses onomatopoeia and alliteration to reflect the sound and movement of someone walking along the road. The poet's evocative depiction of these ghostly figures suggests that no matter how much time passes, the road will never be completely forgotten.

a)   Write down the grade band (4-5, 6-7 or 8-9) that you think this answer falls into.

b)   Give at least two reasons why you chose that grade.

Echo

Walter de la Mare (1873-1956) worked in the **London** offices of the **Anglo-American Oil Company** for eighteen years before becoming a full-time writer. He wrote **poems**, **novels**, **short stories** and **children's literature**.

> Q2   'The Way Through the Woods' and 'Echo' both have a mysterious atmosphere.
> Compare the methods the poets use to create this atmosphere.
>
> **(8 marks)**

Echo

'Who called?' I said, and the words
Through the whispering glades,
Hither, thither, baffled the birds —
    'Who called? Who called?'

5   The leafy boughs on high
        Hissed in the sun;
The dark air carried my cry
        Faintingly on:

Eyes in the green, in the shade,
10   In the motionless brake,
Voices that said what I said,
        For mockery's sake:

'Who cares?' I bawled through my tears:
        The wind fell low:
15   In the silence, 'Who cares? who cares?'
        Wailed to and fro.

Walter de la Mare

Walter de la Mare

Last chance for you to use your sound sense of **judgement** to mark some sample answer extracts. Then you can take that examiner's hat off, safe in the knowledge that you know what they're after come **exam day**.

1

De la Mare and Kipling use rhyme in different ways to make their poems seem mysterious. In 'Echo', the rhyme scheme changes from ABAC in the first stanza to ABAB in the rest of the poem, although de la Mare uses some half-rhymes, such as "shade" / "said" and "tears" / "cares", in stanzas 2-4. This irregularity in the rhyme scheme creates a sense of confusion and uncertainty, which mirrors the narrator's confusion at the mysterious sounds around him. In contrast, 'The Way Through the Woods' has a complex rhyme scheme, which contributes to the mysterious atmosphere of the poem. The last line doesn't fit into this rhyme scheme though, and this makes the end of the poem sound confused and uncertain, as if the mysterious spirits of the people who once travelled along the road are somehow unsettling the narrator.

a) Write down the grade band (4-5, 6-7 or 8-9) that you think this answer falls into.

b) Give at least two reasons why you chose that grade.

2

Both poets use language to create woodland settings in which mysterious, hidden things are happening. In 'Echo', de la Mare's personification of "the whispering glades" makes the woodland seem alive and suggests secretive messages being passed among the trees. His description of "leafy boughs" that "Hissed in the sun" also brings the trees to life, using onomatopoeia and sibilance to evoke the mysterious, threatening noises they make. In a similar way, Kipling uses the secretive behaviour of woodland animals to heighten the mysterious atmosphere of his poem. For example, when "the otter whistles his mate", he seems to be sending a secret message that the reader cannot understand. Similarly, "the trout-ringed pools" contribute to the sense of mystery in the poem, because the rings suggest the presence of the trout, but the fish themselves remain hidden and secret under the water.

a) Write down the grade band (4-5, 6-7 or 8-9) that you think this answer falls into.

b) Give at least two reasons why you chose that grade.

3

Both poems have mysterious sounds in them. In 'Echo' there's the words "Who called? Who called?" and "Who cares? who cares?", that the narrator can hear, but he doesn't know where they're coming from. There's also the sound of "the whispering glades", which seems quite mysterious and uses onomatopoeia to help you imagine it. There's also onomatopoeia in 'The Way Through the Woods', for example "the swish of a skirt". This is quite a mysterious sound, because there isn't actually anyone there, so you don't know where it's coming from and it might be a ghost.

a) Write down the grade band (4-5, 6-7 or 8-9) that you think this answer falls into.

b) Give at least two reasons why you chose that grade.

At Sea — Jennifer Copley

Here's your first **sample exam**. Give yourself **45 minutes** to answer **both questions**. Don't forget, Question 1 is worth **a lot more marks** than Question 2, so you'll want to spend **more time** on your answer to Question 1.

> **Q1** Read the poem below. What do you think the poet is saying about what it can feel like to be left alone? How does the poet present her ideas?
>
> **(24 marks)**

At Sea

With nothing to do now he's gone,
she dusts the house,
sweeps the bleached verandah clear of sand.
The broom leaves a trail of grit on the step,
5   a sprinkling under the hook where it hangs.

A coat for a pillow,
she sleeps downstairs,
dreams the loathed ocean is coming for her,
climbing the cliffs,
10   creeping in through the door.

She wakes to the screaming gulls,
his shirts on the line
and the high tide's breakers'
chill in her arms.

Jennifer Copley

The Watchers — William Stanley Braithwaite

> Q2 'At Sea' and 'The Watchers' both describe the power of the sea.
> Compare the methods the poets use to present the sea in these two poems.
>
> **(8 marks)**

The Watchers

Two women on the lone wet strand
   (*The wind's out with a will to roam*)
The waves wage war on rocks and sand,
   (*And a ship is long due home.*)

5   The sea sprays in the women's eyes —
   (*Hearts can writhe like the sea's wild foam*)
Lower descend the tempestuous skies,
   (*For the wind's out with a will to roam.*)

      "O daughter, thine eyes be better than mine,"
10   (*The waves ascend high as yonder dome*)
"North or south is there never a sign?"
   (*And a ship is long due home.*)

      They watched there all the long night through —
   (*The wind's out with a will to roam*)
15   Wind and rain and sorrow for two —
   (*And heaven on the long reach home.*)

William Stanley Braithwaite

Glossary

strand — the seashore

Don't Say I Said — Sophie Hannah

Just what you've always wanted — another **sample exam**. I know you can't wait to get started, but make sure you **analyse** the poem and jot down a quick **essay plan** before you answer each question.

Q1 Read the poem below. What do you think the poet is saying about the way people react when a relationship ends? How does the poet convey her ideas?

(24 marks)

Don't Say I Said

Next time you speak to you-know-who
I've got a message for him.
Tell him that I have lost a stone
Since the last time I saw him.
5   Tell him that I've got three new books
Coming out soon, but play it
Cool, make it sound spontaneous.
Don't say I said to say it.

He might ask if I've mentioned him.
10   Say I have once, in passing.
Memorize everything he says
And, no, it won't be grassing
When you repeat his words to me –
It's the only way to play it.
15   Tell him I'm toned and tanned and fine.
Don't say I said to say it.

Say that serenity and grace
Have taken root inside me.
My top-note is frivolity
20   But beneath, dark passions guide me.
Tell him I'm radiant and replete
And add that every day it
Seems I am harder to resist.
Don't say I said to say it.

25   Tell him that all my ancient faults
Have been eradicated.
I do not carp or analyse
As I might have when we dated.
Say I'm not bossy any more
30   Or, better still, convey it
Subtly, but get the point across.
Don't say I said to say it.

Sophie Hannah

Flowers — Wendy Cope

Q2   Read the poem below. In both 'Don't Say I Said' and 'Flowers', the narrators reveal
their feelings about the end of a relationship.
What are the similarities and differences in the methods used to describe these feelings?

(8 marks)

Flowers

Some men never think of it.
You did. You'd come along
And say you'd nearly brought me flowers
But something had gone wrong.

5   The shop was closed. Or you had doubts –
The sort that minds like ours
Dream up incessantly. You thought
I might not want your flowers.

It made me smile and hug you then.
10   Now I can only smile.
But, look, the flowers you nearly brought
Have lasted all this while.

Wendy Cope

Answers

Answers

These are only suggested answers — there are lots of different possible answers to these questions. Just make sure that you back up all your points with evidence from the poems.

Section Two — Unseen Poetry Practice

Page 15 — Handbag

Warm-up Questions

1) The narrator is looking through her mother's old handbag.

2) The narrator may be looking through her mother's handbag because her mother has recently died. The smells of the handbag are still strong, suggesting that it was used fairly recently, but the fact that the narrator is looking through it, and the vivid memories evoked by doing so, suggest that her mother is no longer alive.

3) This phrase suggests that the letters were so important to the mother that she filled her handbag with them. It may also hint at the mother's loneliness, suggesting that her life was "crowded" with letters and the memories they contained, rather than being filled with relationships with the people around her.

4) This use of repetition slows the pace of the poem and emphasises the words "womanliness", "love", "anguish" and "war". This shows how important these concepts are in the narrator's memories of her mother, and creates a contrast between the two positive words and the two negative ones.

5) This makes the sentence stand out, so that it catches the eye, even when you just glance at the poem. This technique emphasises the importance of the letters. It suggests that the letters may have dominated the mother's life, making them stand out in the narrator's memories of her, in the same way that this sentence stands out on the page.

6) The poet uses touch to describe the way the narrator's mother treated her husband's letters, and to show how valuable they were to her. The word "softened" shows how often she looked at them, while the verbs "opened" and "refolded" emphasise how carefully she handled them.

7) The poet uses enjambment in the phrase "carried / all through the war". The use of enjambment here emphasises the phrase "all through the war". This highlights the impact of the war on the narrator's mother, and also indicates the importance of these letters to her during the war — perhaps the mother saw them as a sort of charm to ensure her husband would come home.

8) The poem has no regular rhyme scheme, and uses a lot of enjambment, e.g. "The smell / of my mother's handbag". This gives the poem a slow, thoughtful rhythm and makes it seem wistful and melancholy. It creates the impression that the poem records the narrator's train of thought, which makes it seem very personal.

9) The alliteration of the repeated 'l' sounds in "The look of those letters" emphasises the appearance of the letters. This hints at how often they were looked at, highlighting their importance to the narrator and her mother.

Focus on... Mood:

1) a) The poem has a loving, nostalgic mood that is also melancholy and wistful.

   b) The poem shows the mother's love for her husband by emphasising the importance of his letters to her. It also describes the mother's "anguish", which is linked to her husband's absence — possibly his death — during the war. This focus on emotion creates a loving mood, reflecting the mother's feelings for her husband and the narrator's feelings for their mother. The slow rhythm of the poem and the strong memories it describes suggest that the narrator feels sad and wistful as she thinks about her mother.

2) The poet mentions several very distinctive smells, such as "mints", "Coty powder" and "leather" to create a sense of how the handbag smells. These smells bring back fond and vivid memories of the experiences the narrator and her mother went through during the war, which helps to create a nostalgic mood.

3) The poem is written from the viewpoint of a daughter whose mother may have recently died. The first-person perspective makes the poem seem personal, as the memories described show the narrator's affection for their mother and the past. This contributes to the nostalgic mood.

Exam-style Question — Part 1

You'll need to spend about 25 minutes on this, and your answer will probably bring in some of the things you thought about when you answered the other questions on the page. Here are some points you could include in your answer:

- The poet's mother is summed up by the contents of her handbag. The letters that she "carried / all through the war" are still in there, suggesting that they are the most precious thing she owns. This is quite a sad image — perhaps she lost her husband during the war and never got over it.

- The poet uses the senses to evoke memories. The smell of "mints / and lipstick and Coty powder" remind the narrator of her childhood. Specifying the brand of face powder emphasises that this is a memory of a specific person and a specific time period.

- The sense of touch is also very important — the letters are "softened / and worn at the edges", which shows how often they have been read. The three-part list "opened, / read, and refolded so often" emphasises how carefully they were looked at and put away.

- The alliteration in "The look of those letters" creates a rhythm that stresses the word "letters". The word is repeated three times, which shows how important the letters are.

- The placement of "womanliness" at the end of the line separates it from the "love, and anguish, and war" that continue the list. This emphasises that, for the narrator, the smell of her mother's handbag represents much more than the "womanliness" you might expect — it also evokes much stronger memories of her mother's suffering during the war.

- The use of commas and the repetition of "and" in this list slows the pace of the poem and emphasises each idea. The alliteration of the final word of each line particularly stresses

Answers

"womanliness" and "war". This contrasts the mother's natural state with the effect of the war.

Page 17 — Jumper

Warm-up Questions

1) In the poem a man remembers how his mother used to knit in their bomb shelter during the war, and how she used knitting to give her family courage.

2) The narrator says that bombs fell "round our home", so they must have been quite close. The bombs sent "shivers through the walls", reinforcing the image in "walls shake" — the walls physically shook with the impact of the explosions.

3) The narrator's mother made her "scared child" hold the wool as a way of distracting him from the bombs. The child could concentrate on holding the wool instead of the bombs. It also gave the child a strong link with his mother, which would have reassured him.

4) The first emotion in the poem is fear, when the narrator talks about being a "scared child" in the bomb shelter. The second main emotion is the admiration the narrator now feels for his mother's "composure" when she was faced with death. The poet shows these emotions by highlighting his mother's bravery and its effect on him in the past and the present.

5) The poet says the people in the shelter "shivered" and that the bombs made the walls "shiver". This comparison personifies the walls, making it seem like they're also afraid of the bombs.

6) The poet describes the sound ("click of needles") and feel of the shelter ("cold" with walls shaking) which creates a vivid image to help transport the reader into the scene. This is effective because it adds to the sense of fear.

7) The bombs are described as "whistling". This helps the reader imagine the sound of them falling, and the narrator's fear.

8) The rhythm of the poem is quite regular, which brings to mind the rhythmic sound of the narrator's mother knitting.

9) The jumper is "shop-bought" because his mother realised that she was too frail to knit one herself. It is "black", which is the colour of mourning — she knew she would die soon when she bought it. Separating the last line emphasises the contrast with his mother's knitting and recreates the shock of opening the present.

Focus on... Form

1) a) The poem uses a regular ABAB rhyme scheme, with strong rhymes such as "fear"/"hear" and "cold"/"hold".

b) This makes the lines seem controlled, which reflects the way the mother controls her fear for her son's sake.

2) a) The last four lines of the poem are separated from the first twelve lines. They are in two shorter stanzas, each with an uneven number of lines.

b) The separation of the last four lines from the memory in the rest of the poem reflects the difference between the past and the present. The final two stanzas show the mother's continued bravery when she was approaching death.

Exam-style Question — Part 2

You'll need to spend about 15 minutes on this, and your answer will probably bring in some of the things you thought about when you answered the other questions on the two poems. These are some points you could mention:

- In Fainlight's poem, the contents of the handbag represent the narrator's memories of her mother, especially her mother's love for her husband, and her courage in facing the "anguish" of his absence, perhaps his death, during the war. The jumper in Harrison's poem also represents the narrator's mother's courage during the war, as well as her role as a source of comfort and practicality in times of crisis.

- Both poems use the senses to convey vivid memories. In 'Handbag', the poet emphasises the very specific smell of the handbag, while in 'Jumper', the poet uses onomatopoeia to convey the sound of the mother's knitting needles.

- The poems both use repetition. In 'Handbag', repetition of the word "letters" emphasises how important the "Letters from my father" were to the narrator's mother, and how they dominate the narrator's memories of her. Similarly, in 'Jumper', the word "bombs" is repeated at random points, echoing the random explosions of bombs during the war. This shows the danger the family faced and the mother's courage in facing it so "calmly".

- The two poems use form in different ways. The lack of rhyme and use of enjambment in 'Handbag' give the poem a slow rhythm, which sounds wistful and melancholy, reflecting the narrator's sadness when she looks back on her mother's life and the "anguish" she suffered during the war. In contrast, in 'Jumper', the regular rhyme scheme creates an even rhythm, which mirrors the sound of the mother's knitting needles. This emphasises the narrator's admiration for the calm way his mother carried on knitting as "German bombs fell".

Page 19 — 'I Look Into My Glass'

Warm-up Questions

1) The poem is about the contrast between the narrator's ageing body and his emotions, which are still as strong as when he was young.

2) The poet creates a gloomy and reflective mood. He does this by writing from the viewpoint of a narrator who grieves his "wasting" and "fragile" state. This language emphasises the narrator's frailty, while the first-person perspective makes the poem personal as the narrator gloomily reflects on his own approaching death.

3) The narrator's "heart" symbolises his emotions — he wishes that the strong feelings of his youth had faded with his youthful appearance.

4) The poet uses different times of day to represent different phases of the narrator's life. "Noontide" represents his youthful prime, so the "throbbings of noontide" are the strong emotions the narrator felt as a young man and continues to experience now.

Answers

Answers

5) The image of death as "endless rest" almost makes it sound appealing, especially because the narrator is so physically weak. However, the narrator goes on to say that he cannot await death with "equanimity", which shows that, even though his body seems physically ready for this "endless rest", psychologically he is not ready to die.

6) The poet uses the symbolism of different times of day to create contrast between youth and old age, with youth represented by "noontide", while old age is represented by "eve".

7) The poem has a regular rhyme scheme, ABAB, with strong rhymes such as "glass"/"pass" and "skin"/"thin". This gives the poem a regular rhythm that brings to mind the beating of a heart. This reinforces the message that the "throbbings" of emotion are just as strong for the elderly as they are for the young.

8) The poet personifies time as a thief who "steals" the narrator's physical youth without weakening the "throbbings" of his emotions. The idea of time doing this deliberately "to make me grieve" makes the ageing process seem cruel, and emphasises how powerless the narrator is to prevent the physical changes that come with old age.

9) The poet uses caesurae and end-stopping to slow down the pace of the first half of the final stanza, creating a thoughtful, weary tone as the narrator grieves his lost youth. The enjambment in the final lines of the poem increases the pace, suggesting the narrator has a final surge of energy — despite his "fragile frame", he still has the "throbbings" and desires of his youth.

Focus on... Sound

1) a) Alliteration of the 'f' sound is used in "fragile frame".

b) The use of alliteration in "fragile frame" makes this phrase stand out, emphasising the physical fragility that comes with old age. This encourages the reader to empathise with the narrator, and makes it seem unfair that such a frame "shakes" with the "throbbings of noontide".

2) a) Assonance of repeated 'o' sounds is used in "grown cold" and "lonely".

b) The assonance emphasises these words and gives them a sorrowful sound. This highlights the narrator's sadness at how unloved he has become in old age.

Exam-style Question — Part 1

You'll need to spend about 25 minutes on this, and your answer will probably bring in some of the things you thought about when you answered the other questions on the page. Here are some points you could include in your answer:

- The narrator feels frustrated by the contrast between the physical decline that comes with ageing — his "wasting skin" and "fragile frame" — and the powerful "throbbings" of emotion that remain as strong as when he was young. The fact that he feels this way every time he "look[s] into my glass" suggests that this is not just a fleeting feeling, but an emotion he feels regularly.

- Old age is a lonely time for the narrator — the image of "hearts grown cold to me" may suggest that he feels people no longer take an interest in him now that he's old, or it could refer to friends and loved ones who have died, leaving him alone.

- The narrator is distressed by the loss of the people who have "grown cold" to him, and finds it difficult to bear his loneliness calmly, with "equanimity". However, he avoids expressing these feelings directly, perhaps because he is afraid to let such strong emotions shake his "fragile frame", or maybe because he believes that no-one cares how he feels.

- The personification of "Time" as a thief, deliberately stealing the narrator's physical vitality "to make me grieve", makes ageing seem like a cruel process, and suggests the narrator's bitterness at the effects of getting older.

- The phrase "to make me grieve" also points to the suffering that getting older causes the narrator, as does the pitiful metaphor of his "fragile frame" being "shake[n]" by the powerful "throbbings of noontide".

- The form of the poem is very regular. It has a regular rhyme scheme, ABAB, and each stanza has the same pattern of 6 syllables in lines 1, 2 and 4, and 8 syllables in line 3. This gives the poem a strong rhythm like a heartbeat, which mirrors the "throbbings" of the narrator's emotions. However, it also creates a sense of predictability and inevitability, perhaps reflecting the tedious pattern of the narrator's lonely life, and the inevitability of the "endless rest" that he feels he is waiting for.

Page 21 — When You Are Old

Warm-up Questions:

1) The narrator seems to be addressing someone he knows and loves.

2) The narrator is asking the person to imagine the future. He instructs his loved one's future self to look back on their past self. The poem seems to be a warning that if the loved one rejects true love now, they will regret it in old age.

3) The first stanza has a gentle, dream-like mood, created by the use of lots of gentle 's' sounds, e.g. "slowly", "soft", "shadows", and several words associated with sleep, such as "nodding" and "dream". The slow rhythm of the first stanza also contributes to this gentle, sleepy mood.

4) The pace of the first stanza is slow and gentle, reflecting the sort of life that the narrator imagines for the person in old age. The second stanza is brighter and has a slightly faster rhythm, because it describes them as they are now, and the strength of the narrator's love for them.

5) The poem uses a regular ABBA rhyme scheme, with strong rhymes such as "sleep"/"deep" and "book"/"look". The return to the A rhyme at the end of each stanza could reflect how the person addressed in the poem always returns to their memories of their youth. This enclosed rhyme scheme could also suggest that they are trapped by their old age, and cannot recapture the love they once had.

Answers

6) The "glowing bars" represent the metal grate of the fire the person will sit by in old age. The fire offers heat and comfort, but could also represent the warmth of the love that they rejected and now crave. The word "bars" also brings to mind the idea of a prison, suggesting that in old age the person will be trapped by the "glowing bars", while the love they rejected will soar free "amid a crowd of stars".

7) The narrator suggests that his loved one will feel wistful for the loss of their youth — they will "dream" of the way their eyes once looked. The image of the person sitting alone by their fire, "Murmur[ing]" to themselves, suggests that they will be lonely in old age, and will regret rejecting the man who truly loved them — they will think "a little sadly" about him.

8) The narrator's love for the person is personified in the final three lines of the poem. This makes the narrator's love sound important, and reinforces the idea that he is the only man who truly loves them. It also suggests the permanence of the narrator's love — although it has "fled", it is still waiting, hidden among the "stars".

9) The poem has a regular rhyme scheme and is written in iambic pentameter. This gives the poem a slow, steady rhythm, which makes it sound calm and thoughtful, and perhaps mirrors the constancy of the narrator's love for the person they address.

Focus on... Repetition

1) This gives the first stanza a slow rhythm which mirrors the slow pace of life that the narrator envisages for the person in old age. The repetition of "and" also emphasises how numerous the effects of ageing are, which makes them seem endless and inevitable.

2) a) The word "loved" is used in every line of the second stanza.

   b) This illustrates the strength of the narrator's love for the person they are addressing and emphasises the contrast between the narrator, who loves the person's "pilgrim soul", and other men, who only love their "beauty".

Exam-style Question — Part 2

You'll need to spend about 15 minutes on this, and your answer will probably bring in some of the things you thought about when you answered the other questions on the two poems. These are some points you could mention:

- In 'I Look Into My Glass' the narrator describes his own experience of the effects of ageing, whereas in 'When You Are Old', the narrator describes the imagined effects of ageing upon a person he loves.

- Both poems create similar images of the physical decline caused by ageing. In 'I Look Into My Glass', the narrator refers to his "wasting skin" and "fragile frame". Similarly, in 'When You Are Old', the narrator describes the old person as "grey" and "full of sleep", and suggests that their eyes will lose "the soft look" they had when they were young.

- Rhythm is used in both poems to reflect the effects of ageing. In 'I Look Into My Glass', the poet uses lots of punctuation to create a slow rhythm with numerous pauses, which mirrors the elderly narrator's physical weakness and slow, isolated lifestyle. Similarly, the repetition of the word "and" in the first stanza of 'When You Are Old' gives it a slow rhythm, which reflects the slow pace of life that the narrator imagines for the person in old age.

- The poems both depict the loneliness and isolation that can come with old age. In 'I Look Into My Glass', the narrator's isolation is shown by the phrase "hearts grown cold to me". The narrator of 'When You Are Old', meanwhile, claims that, although he loves the person's "changing face", other men only love their "glad grace". This suggests that when the person is "old and grey" and their "beauty" has faded, they will be lonely and isolated because these other men will no longer love them.

Page 23 — The Dead-Beat

Warm-up Questions

1) The poem is about a soldier who has a mental breakdown and dies after being accused of faking his condition.

2) By comparing the man to dead animals, the poet is saying that he isn't being treated like a living creature — he's just "meat".

3) The man's fellow soldiers are willing to kick him when there is clearly something wrong with him. This shows how brutal life in the trenches was, and that the normal rules of how you should treat people didn't apply.

4) There is heavy sarcasm in Owen's choice of these words, usually associated with the behaviour of soldiers in battle, to describe "smiling" uncles and a carefree "young wife" at home. This reminds the reader that those who have never experienced trench warfare have no idea of the horror and suffering it involves, and so have no right to judge "crazed" soldiers like the one in the poem as cowards.

5) The stretcher-bearers "winked", making fun of the man, and agreeing that he must be faking his condition. The doctor calls him "scum" and celebrates his death by saying "Hooray!". These reactions are shocking because medical staff are supposed to care about their patients, but instead they mock him.

6) 'Dead-beat' can mean 'good-for-nothing'. This hints at how the medic and the narrator see the patient — they think he's lazy and useless. It can also mean 'very tired', so the title suggests how exhausted the soldiers were. Looking at the two words separately also hints at what happens in the poem — the soldier dies, and he has been beaten by his situation.

7) There's a lot of rhyme in the poem, but the rhyme scheme is not regular. This could reflect the chaos of war, or the turmoil of the patient's mind.

8) Owen was sympathetic towards soldiers who had breakdowns, but the narrator clearly feels no sympathy for the soldier. He doesn't understand that the man is ill as there is no wound. He and the other soldiers try to "kick him to his feet" and the narrator points a gun at him to make him move.

Focus on... Voice

1) Using direct speech for the different characters brings them to life, and makes the reader feel as if they are witnessing the scene first-hand.

2) a) e.g. "do 'em in", "Blighty", "stiffs"

b) The colloquial language makes the people in the poem seem like ordinary people you would meet day-to-day. This highlights the way that war dehumanises ordinary people and makes them seem callous.

3) People use the word "Hooray!" when they are celebrating, but the poet uses it here to emphasise the fact that there isn't anything to celebrate. It leaves the reader feeling unsettled and confused, as well as horrified and disgusted by the doctor's attitude.

Exam-style Question — Part 1

You'll need to spend about 25 minutes on this, and your answer will probably bring in some of the things you thought about when you answered the other questions on the page. Here are some points you could include in your answer:

• The poem describes the treatment of a soldier who suffers a breakdown while fighting in the trenches. It presents war as a dehumanising experience, which causes people to stop behaving as they would normally be expected to.

• Even though he is ill, the soldier receives no sympathy from his fellow soldiers. Harsh, negative words like "sullenly" and "whined" show that the narrator views him with contempt and does not believe there is anything wrong with him. The other soldiers are equally unsympathetic: they try to "kick him to his feet", the sharp, monosyllabic words emphasising the violence of their behaviour.

• The people who should care for the soldier show him no compassion and view him as "scum". The stretcher-bearers mock him — they "winked" and accuse him of "Malingering". Similarly, the doctor, instead of trying to save his life as you would expect, celebrates his death — he "laugh[s]" and says "Hooray!". This celebratory tone is the opposite of the normal response to death and emphasises the way that war transforms people, so that they no longer behave as they should.

• The brutality of the trenches contrasts with the sarcastic depiction of people at home "smiling ministerially" and having "fun". This suggests that the people at home have no understanding of the horror and suffering of the trenches, and suggests that war can cause soldiers to become angry and resentful towards the people they love at home.

• The form of the poem is very irregular. There is some rhyme, but no regular rhyme scheme, and the length of the stanzas varies. This reflects the violent chaos of conflict, and the chaos and confusion that it has caused in the shell-shocked soldier's mind.

• The use of direct speech and colloquial expressions, such as "I'll do 'em in" and "It's Blighty, p'raps", bring the characters to life and makes the poem seem very real. Because the characters are so life-like, their brutal and inhuman behaviour seems all the more shocking.

Page 25 — Spring in War-Time

Warm-up Questions

1) It's about the narrator's sense of loss after someone she loves dies in the war.

2) She's addressing the person who has died — she uses "your", "our" and "we".

3) The narrator means that she and her lover never got the chance to live together and make a home, because he died.

4) I think the narrator means that all the things she used to love, and enjoyed with her lover, now mean nothing to her because he's not there to enjoy them with her. So she doesn't notice, or can't enjoy, the smell of the violets, because she is overwhelmed by grief.

5) The final line, "On your clay", describes the earth used to fill a grave. The daisies that will grow on the grave haven't yet had time to do so, because it's too recent. The white colour of the daisies may also be reminiscent of funeral flowers, but whilst they carry on living, the person they cover is dead.

6) The rhyme scheme is ABAB. This gives the poem a simple rhythm, which emphasises the sadness of what the narrator is saying.

7) The final line is missing four syllables compared to the other lines. This emphasises it and makes it feel like it finishes too soon, which reflects the relationship between the narrator and her lover — it ended too soon, and now something is missing.

8) I think the final stanza is the most effective in conveying the narrator's emotions, because it sharply contrasts the beauty and gaiety of red roses with the barrenness of the grave, which is a strong image. Also, the final line "On your clay" is shorter than the other lines, which makes it sound almost like the narrator has broken off because she's unable to carry on once she's mentioned death directly.

Focus on... Contrasts

1) The poet contrasts descriptions of spring, in which nature begins to come to life, with the loss and regret that the narrator experiences after the death of her lover.

2) The narrator repeats the central contrast in each stanza. The first few lines of each stanza describe the joy of spring and rebirth with phrases like "Every bird has heart to sing". However, the final line of each stanza shifts the focus to the regret and loss the narrator feels over her lover's death. This emphasises the contrast between new life and the narrator's loss.

3) This contrast makes the reader feel sorry for the narrator — she is unable to appreciate the beauty around her, as she feels only loss, rather than joy.

Exam-style Question — Part 2

You'll need to spend about 15 minutes on this, and your answer will probably bring in some of the things you thought about when you answered the other questions on the two poems. These are some points you could mention:

• 'The Dead-Beat' describes the effects of war upon men fighting in the trenches, using sarcasm to suggest that people at home are untouched by the conflict. In contrast, 'Spring in War-Time' vividly conveys the suffering that conflict can cause for people at home.

- Both poems show the personal effect of war on particular individuals. In 'The Dead-Beat', this is achieved through the use of direct speech, which brings individual characters to life and conveys their varied responses to the violence and suffering of war. In 'Spring in War-Time', however, the poet conveys the personal effects of war by focusing on just one individual, and writing from her perspective about the effects of the loss of a loved one in conflict.

- In contrasting ways, both poets use form to convey the effects of war. 'The Dead-Beat' does not have a regular rhyme scheme, nor a regular rhythm. This makes the poem seem confused and chaotic, reflecting the chaos caused by war. 'Spring in War-Time', on the other hand, has a very regular rhyme scheme and rhythm, except that the last line is four syllables shorter than all the others. The cutting short of this line symbolises the cutting short of the narrator's lover's life, and the way that his death has interrupted the rhythm of the narrator's life.

- The two poets use very different language to create contrasting effects. In 'The Dead-Beat', harsh, ugly similes comparing the soldier to "a cod" and "meat" show the dehumanising effect of war on those fighting. In 'Spring in War-Time', by contrast, the poet uses beautiful, vivid depictions of nature (e.g. "the sprinkled blackthorn snow") to stress the difference between the past and the present and show how much happier things were before the war.

Page 27 — The Bereavement of the Lion-Keeper

Warm-up Questions

1) The poem is about an old zookeeper, who stays on to look after a lion in the zoo after it has closed.

2) The keeper stayed "long after his pay stopped," suggesting that the zoo had closed, and he stayed on out of love for the lion. Even though he was hungry himself ("times grew hungrier"), the keeper still begged for food for the lion, not for himself.

3) The stanzas beginning with "Who" reflect the keeper's certainty about his life, and the rhythm of his daily routine. The final stanza starts with a lower case "but". It also uses enjambment and marks the change of subject to how the keeper is struggling to accept the lion's death and "knows no way to let go". This emphasises the impact of the lion's death on the lion keeper, showing how the bereavement has destroyed the rhythm of his daily life.

4) This means that the lion that the keeper had watched so regularly is no longer sleeping, but has died of old age.

5) This suggests that, even with bombs falling, the keeper and the lion still felt safe because they were together.

6) "Deepest purr in the world", "plunge fingers / into rough glowing fur", "wrapped in his warmth" and "pungent scent" create a strong image of the sound, feel and smell of the lion. They give the impression of a gentle, loving, mutual relationship, even though man is expected to be afraid of lions, and lions are predators.

7) a) Both the lion and the old man are "moth-eaten" and "growing old together", and when in the second stanza the keeper "begged for meat" that needed to be "cut... up small to feed him" it could be referring to the lion and the man, too.

b) It makes the reader pity the old man, who was living in poverty and struggling to survive. It also suggests that, after the lion dies, the old man probably won't have long to live.

8) You are left with a feeling that the old man doesn't have much to look forward to, as he walks "out of sunlight" and becomes "an old man in a city", as though he has no identity without the lion. Also, the idea that "elderly lions / were not immortal" hints that humans aren't either. But there is hope in the idea that humans can be kind, caring, loving and loyal.

9) The final stanza really puts across how lost the keeper feels without the lion, that he knew "no way

to let go / of love"; his love of the lion is compared to "sunlight", and when the lion dies he is in the dark. The final short line "without a lion" emphasises his feeling of loss.

Focus on... Tone

1) a) The poem has a tone of respect and admiration at the simple, but profound love between the lion and his devoted keeper.

b) The repetition of "Who", especially at the start of the first five stanzas, gradually builds a sense of admiration at the keeper's devotion to the lion. Phrases such as "who knew" and "who has heard" emphasise the keeper's impressive knowledge and bond with the lion, adding to the tone of respect.

2) In the final stanza, the tone becomes sorrowful as the poet describes how the keeper is lost after the lion's death. There is a strong sense of pain, loss and helplessness as the keeper "knows no way" to let go of the lion or live without him.

Exam-style Question — Part 1

You'll need to spend about 25 minutes on this, and your answer will probably bring in some of the things you thought about when you answered the other questions on the page. Here are some points you could include in your answer:

- The poem describes the close, loving relationship between the zookeeper and the lion, suggesting that sometimes the relationship between a person and an animal can be as close as that between two people.

- The poet emphasises the zookeeper's loyalty to the lion. Even though "his pay stopped" and he is in danger from "bombs", he stays with the lion and cares for him. The use of emotive words (e.g. "begged") and imagery (e.g. "as times grew hungrier") highlight the hardship that the man endured for the sake of the lion.

- The poet uses onomatopoeia (e.g. "purr") and appeals to the senses (e.g. "rough glowing fur", "pungent scent") to demonstrate the mutual affection and trust between the lion and the keeper, who remained together throughout the war, feeling safe because they were together.

Answers

- The imagery in the poem suggests that, for the zookeeper, the lion represents a family he lost, or perhaps never had. The image of the keeper and the lion "growing old together" almost makes the pair sound like a married couple, something that is reinforced by the description of them "curled close" together. The way the zookeeper cuts the lion's food "small to feed him", meanwhile, creates an image of the lion as an infant, being fed by its father.

- The final stanza shows the depth of grief the man feels when the lion dies. The old man "knows no way to let go" of his love for the lion, and doesn't know how to go on without him. This stanza shows that the keeper's identity is so tied up with his role looking after the lion, that when the lion dies, he no longer knows who he is — he doesn't know how to live "in a city / without a lion". This makes his grief and loss even more profound, because, as well as losing his closest companion, he has also lost his own identity.

- The poem is written in the third person, but often seems to be speaking from the keeper's perspective. This emphasises the comfort and companionship that the lion gave the keeper, and makes his love and pain more real and pitiable.

Page 29 — The Tyger

Warm-up Questions

1) This poem is about the nature of the tiger and its creator, and the narrator's wonder that a single creator could make something so beautiful yet so terrifying.

2) The narrator admires and fears the tiger. He describes the tiger's "fearful symmetry" — he is frightened by it, but also inspired by its beauty.

3) The narrator contrasts the "bright" tiger with the darkness of the "night". This juxtaposition emphasises the tiger's beauty by illustrating that the animal stands out against the dark.

4) Only mentioning parts of the tiger's creator makes the creator sound more mysterious — he can't be fully known or understood.

5) The poem asks lots of questions and doesn't give any answers. This is very effective because it reflects the fact that however much we try to find out about the creator, we will not get any answers. It creates a tone of amazement and wonder too.

6) There is alliteration in "what dread grasp / Dare its deadly terrors clasp?" This emphasises "dread", "Dare" and "deadly", which adds to the impression that the narrator fears both the tiger and its creator.

7) The rhythm of the poem is very regular. This brings to mind the rhythmic hammering of a blacksmith as he beats metal into shape, so it reinforces the main image of the poem.

8) The poet is asking whether the same creator could have created the tiger as well as the lamb. This raises questions about what kind of creator could make something as innocent as a lamb, and something as dangerous as a tiger. The contrast between the two animals makes the tiger seem even more frightening. In the Bible, Jesus is referred to as the 'Lamb of God', so the lamb may also represent Jesus.

9) a) It reminds the reader that the original question of who created the tiger has still not been answered.

b) The first stanza asks who "Could" make the tiger — who has the ability. The last stanza asks instead who would "Dare" make the tiger — this reinforces the power and mystery of a creator who has the courage to make such a creature.

Focus on... Imagery

1) a) The poet describes the tiger as "burning bright".

b) This fire imagery paints a vivid picture of the "bright" fur of the tiger in the dark forest. It also gives a sense of the power of the tiger, making it seem more beautiful and more dangerous.

2) a) The poet personifies the stars throwing "down their spears" and watering "heaven with their tears".

b) This personification emphasises the tiger's power, as it is so fearsome that even the stars do not dare to face it. This makes the reader question the creator's motives in making such a creature.

3) I think the image of the creator as a blacksmith is very effective. You get a sense of a powerful man straining to shape the various parts of the tiger. The strength of the blacksmith represents the power of the creator.

Exam-style Question — Part 2

You'll need to spend about 15 minutes on this, and your answer will probably bring in some of the things you thought about when you answered the other questions on the two poems. These are some points you could mention:

- Both poems present a sense of admiration and respect for the animals they describe. The hyperbolic description of the lion's purr as "the deepest purr in the world" makes the lion sound extraordinary and shows the narrator's respect for him. In 'The Tyger', meanwhile, the narrator's admiration for the tiger is conveyed through images such as "thy fearful symmetry", and by the use of repeated rhetorical questions, which suggest that the tiger is so impressive that the narrator cannot fully comprehend it.

- Metaphors relating to light are used in both poems to convey the animals' power and beauty. Sheenagh Pugh refers to the lion's "rough glowing fur", while Blake describes the tiger as "burning bright" and refers to "the fire" of its eyes.

- Blake uses the extended metaphor of a blacksmith's forge to emphasise the power of the creator who made the tiger and, by extension, the power of the tiger itself. In contrast, although Pugh does convey the lion's power and beauty, she also stresses that the animal is "not immortal", the metaphorical depiction of it as "moth-eaten" emphasising its frailty.

- The poems both use alliteration, but to very different effect. In 'The Tyger', the use of alliteration in the question "what dread grasp / Dare its deadly terrors clasp?" emphasises the narrator's fear of the tiger. In Pugh's poem, however, there is no fear in the zookeeper's attitude towards the lion. Instead, the alliterative phrase "curled close" highlights the closeness and trust between them.

Answers

Page 31 — A century later

Warm-up Questions

1) The poem is about a schoolgirl who survives being shot in the head and, by doing so, earns the right to a normal life. Her actions inspire other schoolgirls to stand up for their education.

2) The poet describes female education with an extended metaphor of war — the "school-bell is a call to battle" and "every step to class" is "a step into the firing-line". This makes education for women seem dangerous, but shows it is a cause that is worth fighting for.

3) This description emphasises the schoolgirl's youth and vulnerability. This makes the idea that she is a "target" even more shocking.

4) This shows the girl's strength and defiance in the face of oppression and danger — she bravely stands up to her attackers by calling the bullet *stupid* for attempting to stop female education.

5) a) The mood of the poem is initially tense, but it becomes more defiant and hopeful towards the end.

   b) The poet uses military language to create a tense and dangerous mood. Attending a "class" is described as going into the "firing-line", showing how dangerous the fight for female education is. Later, the military language used to describe the girls taking "their place on the front line" creates a determined mood. There is a sense that what they are doing is dangerous but extremely important for the future.

6) The poet uses sibilance in the phrase "Surrendered, surrounded, she". The similar sounds of "surrendered" and "surrounded" increase the feeling that the girl is trapped. The sibilance also highlights the moment she is shot, which is a key event in the poem.

7) a) The poem describes the path of the bullet with idyllic imagery to do with nature — as she is shot, she visualises "an orchard / in full bloom".

   b) This juxtaposition between the shooting and the beautiful imagery emphasises the girl's strength and resilience — she takes something positive from the brutal, frightening reality of the shooting.

8) The poet personifies the bullet when the schoolgirl addresses it as if it were human, telling it *"you are stupid"* and *"You have failed"*. This personification makes the bullet a stand-in for the girl's attackers and all those who want to silence her or stop female education. By addressing the bullet directly, the girl responds defiantly to her attackers and opponents.

Focus on... Punctuation

1) The poem uses a caesura after "and walks on" to reflect how the bullet hits its target, but fails to destroy the girl. The bullet was intended to stop her, but the caesura makes the reader pause and take note of the fact that she has walked on instead of being stopped.

2) a) The poet breaks the girl's speech into short sentences with full stops, such as "You have failed."

   b) This makes the girl's defiant protest sound blunt and forceful.

3) The enjambment creates a sense of momentum. This reflects the growing number of schoolgirls fighting for their education, who multiply from a "murmur" to a "swarm".

Exam-style Question — Part 1

You'll need to spend about 25 minutes on this, and your answer will probably bring in some of the things you thought about when you answered the other questions on the page. Here are some points you could include in your answer:

- The poem describes the fight for female education through the example of a schoolgirl who is shot in the head but survives. This suggests that standing up for female education is dangerous and difficult, but ultimately rewarding and necessary.

- The poet emphasises the dangerous nature of the fight for female education through an extended metaphor of war, in which the "school-bell" becomes a "call to battle", and going to "class" is going into the "firing-line". The events of the poem suggest that this is not simply a metaphor — the schoolgirl actually is a "target" who is shot at.

- The poet uses sibilance to highlight how unbalanced the fight for female education is. The description "Surrendered, surrounded" uses repeated sounds to emphasise how the girl is trapped in a dangerous situation. The idea that she has been "surrounded" suggests that the forces opposing her education are enormous and overwhelming, which shows the extent of the obstacles she must overcome to receive an education.

- The poet uses imagery of nature to highlight the opportunities that fighting for female education brings. When the bullet hits her head, it reveals an "orchard / in full bloom" and a field that is "humming" and "full of poppies" in the girl's mind. The fruit in the orchard could represent knowledge, so this imagery shows that the bullet ironically brings life and opportunities, rather than death. This could illustrate how the schoolgirl's survival inspires a generation of girls to fight for their right to education.

- The poem shifts towards a defiant tone in the second half, as the poet describes how the girl has "won / the right to be ordinary". The poet uses a triplet of verb phrases, "wear bangles", "paint her fingernails" and "go to school", to describe the opportunities that have opened up to the girl due to her efforts. Although these may seem like trivial things, their everyday nature emphasises the oppression some women face, denied basic rights such as education. This shows that the fight for female education is necessary and important.

- The use of direct speech, in which the schoolgirl addresses the bullet that hit her, shows how the fight for female education gives women who have been silenced a voice. Although the bullet wanted to silence her, her education enables her to recognise that it is *"stupid"* and a failure. This emphasises the power of education, which is further reinforced by the schoolgirl continuing to use her voice to fight for it.

Answers

- The final stanza suggests that the tide is turning in the fight for female education — the cause, which was once a quiet "murmur", becomes a "swarm" as schoolgirls join "one by one". This imagery of progression highlights the building momentum behind the cause, which is reflected by enjambment.

Page 33 — History Lesson

Warm-up Questions

1) The poem describes a photograph of the narrator standing on the beach as a child, and contrasts it with a photograph of her grandmother on the same beach forty years earlier.

2) The enjambment between the lines "The sun cuts / the rippling Gulf in flashes with each / tidal rush" reflects the movement of the waves breaking on the shore, which helps to bring the scene to life.

3) I think the poet chose this title because the poem teaches the reader about how the experience of being a black or mixed-race woman has changed over time. I think it is an effective title because it highlights how recent the "History" of oppression is and the importance of learning a "Lesson" from it.

4) The simile of minnows "glinting like switchblades" emphasises the flashing, silver colour of the fish, but it also introduces a sense of violence and danger which reflects the persecution of black and mixed-race people.

5) Both the narrator and her grandmother stand with their "hands on the flowered hips" of their outfits. Whereas the narrator stands on "a wide strip" of beach, her grandmother could only stand on "a narrow plot" of sand, because there were specific areas that *colored* people had to stay in.

6) These lines suggest that the narrator was born at a time of hope and change. The beach was "opened" to black and mixed-race people, who the narrator refers to as "us", two years before the photograph was taken. The verb "opened" hints that the narrator will have more opportunities in her lifetime than her grandmother did.

7) The poet uses alliteration of 'b' in the phrase "bright bikini". These repeated plosive sounds place emphasis on the narrator's outfit, highlighting how modern and unrestrictive it is compared to her grandmother's traditional "cotton meal-sack dress".

8) The description of how the narrator's toes "curl around wet sand" appeals to the sense of touch, making the seaside scene seem very vivid.

9) Yes, I think the narrator admires her grandmother because she affectionately describes her "smiling", despite being limited to a small stretch of sand due to her skin colour. There is a sense that her grandmother made the most of what she had, despite the prejudice she faced.

Focus on... Structure

1) The poem is roughly structured into two parts. In the first part, the narrator describes a photograph of herself as a child, and in the second part, she describes a photograph of her grandmother forty years earlier.

2) The poem begins by plunging the reader into the narrator's memories, with the phrase "I am four in this photograph". This instantly grabs the reader's attention by painting a clear image of the narrator's childhood.

3) a) The narrator first describes a photograph of herself and then describes a photograph of her grandmother. This structure highlights the way both subjects enjoy the same activities, even though the photographs are taken years apart.

b) The poem's structure invites comparisons between the time periods in the two photographs. The narrator wears a "bright bikini" compared to her grandmother's "cotton meal-sack dress". Their experience of the beach is also strikingly different — the narrator has access to the whole beach, whereas segregation means that her grandmother can only stand on a "narrow" patch.

Exam-style Question — Part 2

You'll need to spend about 15 minutes on this, and your answer will probably bring in some of the things you thought about when you answered the other questions on the two poems. These are some points you could mention:

- Both poets use figurative language to illustrate the dangers that are faced when overcoming inequalities in society. Dharker uses an extended metaphor of war to describe the classroom as a "front line" in which girls are soldiers but also potentially targets. Trethewey compares fish swimming around the narrator's feet to "switchblades", which hints that the narrator may still be in danger, even though inequalities have been reduced.

- In both poems, the victory over enormous inequalities is described in a way that seems insignificant on the surface. Dharker describes the schoolgirl winning her fight for education as simply winning "the right to be ordinary", such as the ability to "paint her fingernails", whilst Trethewey describes the end of segregation through the image of the narrator enjoying a "wide strip" of beach, compared to her grandmother's "narrow plot / of sand". Through these examples, both poems show that these 'ordinary' things should be rights, not privileges.

- The poems use enjambment to similar effect. In 'A century later', Dharker uses enjambment at the end of the poem to reflect the momentum building in the fight for female education. In 'History Lesson', Trethewey uses enjambment throughout to suggest the way that change is gathering pace through the passing of time.

- Both poems depict ordinary people overcoming terrible inequalities in society. However, whereas the narrator in Trethewey's poem experiences fewer inequalities than her grandmother, whose experience acts as a "History Lesson" for readers, Dharker's poem is set in the present day and uses the present tense to suggest that the fight for female education is just beginning.

Answers

Section Three — Marking Sample Answers

Page 37 — Composed Upon Westminster Bridge

1) a) 4-5
   b) Two from, e.g.:
   • It addresses the question and makes a valid point about the narrator's feelings.
   • The argument is supported by some relevant examples from the poem.
   • The examples are not explained or analysed in very much detail.
   • It does not use enough technical terms.

2) a) 8-9
   b) Two from, e.g.:
   • It makes an interesting suggestion about the poet's use of personification.
   • It correctly identifies the form of the poem and explains its significance.
   • It uses a wide range of technical terms.

3) a) 6-7
   b) Two from, e.g.:
   • It explores the poet's use of language well.
   • It uses several relevant examples from the poem.
   • It uses technical terms accurately.
   • Some of the quotes are too long, and not well integrated into the argument.
   • The point about the personification of the city could be developed further.

Page 39 — London

1) a) 8-9
   b) Two from, e.g.:
   • It convincingly compares the way the two poets use form to create contrasting atmospheres.
   • The argument is supported well with examples from both poems.
   • It uses a range of technical terms.

2) a) 6-7
   b) Two from, e.g.:
   • This gives a thoughtful comparison of the poets' use of language.
   • It explains the effect of some examples from both poems.
   • It uses technical terms accurately.
   • Some of the examples are not explained at all.

3) a) 4-5
   b) Two from, e.g.:
   • It compares the poets' use of language.
   • It uses quotes from the poems and gives some explanation of their effect on the reader.
   • The comparison between the two poems could be developed further.
   • It only uses one technical term.

Page 41 — Eating Poetry

1) a) 4-5
   b) Two from, e.g.:
   • It makes a valid point in response to the question.
   • It uses plenty of quotes to support the argument
   • The quotes aren't explored or analysed in detail.
   • It doesn't use many technical terms.

2) a) 8-9
   b) Two from, e.g.:
   • It presents a convincing, well-developed argument about the role of the librarian in the poem.
   • It uses a range of examples from the poem to support the argument.
   • It gives an insightful analysis of the techniques used.
   • It uses a wide range of technical terms correctly.

3) a) 6-7
   b) Two from, e.g.:
   • It gives a thoughtful analysis of the imagery used in the poem.
   • It shows a good understanding of some of the themes in the poem.
   • It uses technical terms correctly.
   • The point about the dogs is interesting, but could be developed further.

Page 43 — Volumes

1) a) 8-9
   b) Two from, e.g.:
   • This gives a detailed comparison of the form of the two poems.
   • It compares the effect that the poets' techniques have on the reader.
   • It uses several different technical terms accurately.

2) a) 6-7
   b) Two from, e.g.:
   • It makes some good comparisons between the language used in the two poems, using relevant examples.
   • It highlights similarities in the way the poets use language.
   • It does not use many technical terms.
   • It needs some more in-depth analysis of specific language features.

3) a) 4-5
   b) Two from, e.g.:
   • It makes several valid comparisons between the two poems.
   • The first two points are supported by relevant examples from both poems, but the final point needs an example from 'Eating Poetry' to back it up.
   • None of the points are very well explained or developed. It would be better to focus on one point in detail, rather than covering lots of different points very briefly.
   • It needs to use more technical terms.

Page 45 — The Way Through the Woods

1) a) 4-5
   b) Two from, e.g.:
   • This addresses the question.
   • It uses plenty of quotes to back up points, but these aren't analysed in very much detail.
   • It only uses one technical term.
   • It would have been good to mention the alliteration and sibilance of "swish" and "skirt".

Answers

62

2) a) 6-7

b) Two from, e.g.:
• It uses several well-chosen examples to support the argument.
• It explores some of the techniques the poet has used and the effects they create.
• It needs to analyse the effect of specific language features in more detail.
• It uses some technical terms.

3) a) 8-9

b) Two from, e.g.:
• It analyses several language features in detail.
• It explores the way the poet's techniques affect the reader.
• It explains the significance of the ghostly figures on the road.
• It uses a variety of technical terms.

Page 47 — Echo

1) a) 6-7

b) Two from, e.g.:
• It shows a good understanding of the form of the two poems.
• It explains the effect of the poets' techniques on the reader.
• It uses appropriate technical terms.
• There is some comparison of the two poems, but the similarities and differences need to be explored more fully.

2) a) 8-9

b) Two from, e.g.:
• It makes thoughtful comments on the imagery used in both poems.
• It shows a good understanding of the techniques the poets have used, and their effect on the reader.
• It uses a range of examples from both poems to support the argument.
• It uses several technical terms.

3) a) 4-5

b) Two from, e.g.:
• It compares the poets' use of sound.
• It uses relevant examples from both poems and gives some explanation of them.
• The examples could be explored in more detail.
• It only uses one technical term.

Section Four — Practice Exam Questions

Page 48 — At Sea

1)
• The poem is about a woman who is left behind when her partner goes to sea.
• The poem has a nightmarish quality — the woman is alone, waiting nervously for her husband's safe return. The atmosphere is tense, as if something bad may be about to happen. The second stanza deals with the woman's actual nightmare, and the alliterative words "coming", "climbing" and "creeping" make the sea feel very menacing and hostile. It's like someone creeping in and stealing her lover. She wakes up, but with the "screaming gulls" and the sea "chill in her arms" it still feels as if she's in a nightmare.
• The main feeling of the first stanza is boredom — she has "nothing to do now he's gone". She needs to keep busy, so she cleans the house. But the cleaning is futile; the broom "leaves a trail of grit". This could show that the act of cleaning can't cleanse her mind of her fear and anxiety.
• The first stanza contains lots of 's' sounds — "dusts", "sweeps", "sand", "step", "sprinkling" and "hangs". This makes the stanza feel longer, reflecting the woman's feelings about how time slows down whilst she's alone. The sibilance also sounds like the sea, so it's a constant reminder of the woman's enemy.
• The second stanza describes the woman going to bed. She "sleeps downstairs", perhaps because she can't bear to be alone in their shared bed. This shows how even small things can be a painful reminder of the person you're missing. She also uses a "coat for a pillow" — the coat could well be her partner's, and by sleeping with it she may feel closer to him.

• In the third stanza, the onomatopoeic "screaming gulls" creates a vivid image. It's also a stark contrast to the silence of the rest of the poem, where the only sounds are the sweeping of the broom and the sibilance of the sea creeping closer. The screaming gulls might also be reminiscent of the screams of drowning sailors, highlighting the woman's fear that her partner will die at sea.
• His shirts are hanging on the washing line, which is a reminder that he's coming back, and feels homely and hopeful for a moment. But the final two lines, "and the high tide's breakers' / chill in her arms", immediately recall the sea and the woman's constant fear that her partner will never return. The "chill" of the waves in the woman's arms seems like a forewarning of death — as if she's holding her partner's cold, drowned body in her arms.
• The structure of the poem, broken into three stanzas, mimics the structure of the woman's life whilst her partner is away — it's divided into day, night, day. There's no rhyme, which reflects her own slightly panicky state of mind. The final stanza is heavily enjambed, which creates a feeling of time moving faster, of disorder and confusion. The final stanza is also a line shorter, possibly reflecting her partner's early death.

Page 49 — The Watchers

2)
• Both poems present the sea as something dangerous and powerful. The subject of 'At Sea' fears that her partner will die at sea, while in 'The Watchers', the fact that the ship the women are waiting for is *long due* implies it has been wrecked.
• Both poets use language to convey the sounds of the sea. In 'The Watchers', the repetition of the alliterative line "*the wind's out with a will to roam*" mirrors the sound of the waves. The repeated 'w' sound on alternating syllables creates a rhythmic effect which reflects the relentless power of the sea. Similarly, in 'At Sea', the sibilance in the first stanza (e.g. "she dusts the house, / sweeps") echoes the sound of the sea and suggests its inescapable presence.

Answers

- The poets both create tense, frightening atmospheres through the imagery they use. For example, the onomatopoeic image of "screaming gulls" in 'At Sea' creates tension and anxiety by suddenly breaking the silence of the poem with a sound that suggests fear and suffering. In 'The Watchers', the imagery of the "tempestuous skies" and the waves that *"ascend high as yonder dome"* creates a sense of danger and the power of nature.

- The two poets personify the sea. Copley depicts it "coming", "climbing" and "creeping", whereas Braithwaite describes how the "waves wage war" on the beach. In both cases, the imagery the poets use and the alliterative 'c' and 'w' sounds make the sea sound menacing and unstoppable.

- The form of each poem is very different, and is used to create different effects. 'At Sea' is written in free verse, with variable line lengths and no rhyme, which makes it seem unstructured and chaotic. This reflects the way the sea affects the woman, mirroring the lack of structure in her life when her partner is away at sea. In contrast, the form of 'The Watchers' reflects the movement of the sea. Unlike 'At Sea', Braithwaite's poem has a regular rhyme scheme, ABAB, which creates a strong rhythm, mirroring the relentless movement of the waves.

Page 50 — Don't Say I Said

1)

- In the poem, the narrator obsessively instructs a friend in exactly what information to pass on to an ex-partner.

- The poem is written as a monologue; the end-stopped double rhymes (e.g. "convey it" / "say it") on the odd lines increase the pace of the poem, giving the impression that there is no opportunity for the listener to speak. This, together with the repetition of "I" illustrates the egotism that can follow the breakdown of a relationship.

- Double rhymes like "play it" / "say it" force the reader to spit out the word "it", giving the poem an angry, frustrated tone. This reflects the fact that, despite her insistence that she's "toned and tanned and fine", the narrator still feels angry and upset about the end of the relationship.

- The narrator pays no attention to whether her friend is comfortable lying for her (e.g. the ironic order "Say I'm not bossy any more") or "repeat[ing] his words". This shows how the breakdown of a relationship can create conflict, with one or both parties trying to make mutual friends take sides.

- The poet uses enjambment to emphasise the narrator's desire to "play it / Cool" and "convey it / Subtly". The emphasis on the words "Cool" and "Subtly" creates irony; the narrator is desperate for her former partner to know how well she is doing, but equally desperate for him not to know that she wants to impress him. This is highlighted by the refrain "Don't say I said to say it", which sounds forced and unnatural, much like the image she wants to present.

- The form of the poem mimics the content: on the surface it seems light and playful, but the careful rhymes (e.g. "inside me" / "guide me") reveal how much the narrator cares. Even though she wants to appear "replete" without her former partner, the poem suggests that he is all she can think about.

- The poem has a slightly awkward rhythm, created by the forced rhymes and enjambment of lines such as "And add that every day it / Seems I am harder to resist". This highlights the fact that the narrator's desperation to come across well makes her clumsy and awkward, and shows how the breakdown of a relationship can bring out the worst in people.

Page 51 — Flowers

2)

- The narrators of the two poems feel differently about the end of their relationships. While the narrator of 'Don't Say I Said' seems angry and hurt, the narrator of 'Flowers' seems much calmer, conveying a positive view of her former partner, and a sense of wistful regret about the end of their relationship.

- The poems both have a conversational style, using short sentences, simple language and enjambment. This gives them both a direct, personal tone, reflecting the very personal feelings that they present.

- The two poems use language to present contrasting attitudes towards the former partner. In 'Don't Say I Said', the narrator refers to her ex-partner as "you-know-who", using monosyllabic words to create a sense of anger and aggression. This colloquial phrase conveys the narrator's anger towards her ex-partner, suggesting that she is so upset that she cannot even bring herself to say his name. In 'Flowers', on the other hand, the narrator presents a positive view of her former partner. The short, simple sentence "You did." stresses his thoughtfulness, while repetition of the word "smile" in the final stanza shows that, even though the relationship has come to an end, the narrator still views it in a positive light.

- The narrator of 'Don't Say I Said' refers to her ex-partner in the third person ("him"), which creates a sense of distance between the former couple. This suggests that, despite the narrator's belief that "He might ask" about her, the connection they once had has now been lost. In contrast, there is a sense of connection between the narrator of 'Flowers' and her former partner, created by the use of the second person ("you") to refer to him, and phrases such as "minds like ours", which suggest that the pair still have things in common.

- The two poems are very different in rhythm and tone, reflecting the narrators' contrasting feelings about the end of their relationships. The end-stopped double rhymes in 'Don't Say I Said' give the poem a frustrated tone, which shows how angry and upset the narrator feels about the end of the relationship. In contrast, 'Flowers' uses gentle rhymes like "ours" / "flowers", and this, combined with the poem's short sentences and simple language, gives the poem a calm, gentle tone. This reflects the narrator's positive view of her ex-partner, but it also makes the narrator seem sad and wistful, conveying her feelings of regret that the relationship has come to an end.

Glossary

alliteration	Where words that are close together **start** with the **same sound**, e.g. "fragile frame".
ambiguity	Where a word or phrase has **two or more** possible **meanings**.
assonance	When words share the same **vowel sound** but the consonants are different, e.g. "stamp her **fe**et and w**ee**p".
ballad	A form of **poetry** that tells a **story** and can often be set to **music**.
blank verse	Poetry written in iambic pentameter that **doesn't rhyme**.
caesura	A **pause** in a line, e.g. after the word "dropped" in "He dropped, — more sullenly than wearily".
colloquial	Sounding like everyday **spoken** language, e.g. "it won't be grassing".
consonance	**Repetition** of a **consonant sound** in nearby words, e.g. "A murmur, a swarm".
contrast	When two things are described in a way which emphasises **how different** they are. E.g. a poet might contrast two different people or two different voices.
direct speech	The **actual words** that are said by someone.
dramatic monologue	A **form** of poetry that uses the assumed voice of a **single speaker** who is **not the poet** to address an **implied audience**, e.g. 'Don't Say I Said'.
emotive	Something that makes you **feel** a particular **emotion**.
empathy	When someone **understands** what someone else is experiencing and how they **feel** about it.
end-stopping	Finishing a line of poetry with the **end** of a **phrase or sentence**.
enjambment	When a sentence or phrase runs over from **one line** or **stanza** to the **next**.
euphemism	An **indirect** term for something **upsetting** or **offensive**, e.g. "On your clay" is used to avoid referring directly to death or a grave in 'Spring in War-Time'.
first person	When someone writes about themselves or their group, using words like **"I"**, **"my"**, **"we"** and **"our"**.
form	The **type** of poem, e.g. a sonnet or a ballad, and its **features**, like number of lines, rhyme and rhythm.
free verse	Poetry that **doesn't rhyme** and has **no regular rhythm**.
half-rhymes	Words that have a **similar**, but not identical, **end sound**. E.g. "shade" and "said".
hyperbole	An **exaggerated** statement that is **not** meant to be taken **literally**.
iambic pentameter	Poetry with a **metre** of **ten syllables** — five of them stressed, and five unstressed. The **stress** falls on **every second syllable**, e.g. "When **you** are **old** and **grey** and **full** of **sleep**".
iambic tetrameter	Like iambic pentameter but with a metre of **eight** syllables — four stressed and four unstressed. E.g. "The **waves** wage **war** on **rocks** and **sand**".
imagery	Language that creates a **picture in your mind**. It includes **metaphors**, **similes** and **personification**.
internal rhyme	When two or more words **rhyme**, and at least one of the words **isn't** at the end of a line. The rhyming words can be in the **same** line or **nearby** lines, e.g. "It is **underneath** the coppice and **heath**".
irony	When **words** are used in a **sarcastic** or **comic** way to **imply the opposite** of what they normally mean. It can also mean when there is a difference between **what people expect** and **what actually happens**.
juxtaposition	When a poet puts two ideas, events, characters or descriptions **close to each other** to encourage the reader to **contrast** them. E.g. the excited narrator and the terrified librarian in 'Eating Poetry'.
language	The **choice of words** used. Different kinds of language have **different effects**.
layout	The way a piece of poetry is visually **presented** to the reader, e.g. line length, whether the poem is broken up into different stanzas, whether lines create some kind of visual pattern.
metaphor	A way of describing something by saying that it **is something else**, e.g. "the fire of thine eyes".

Glossary

metre	The arrangement of stressed and unstressed syllables to create **rhythm** in a line of poetry.
mood	The **feel** or **atmosphere** of a poem, e.g. humorous, threatening, eerie.
narrative	Writing that tells a **story**.
narrator	The **voice** speaking the words. E.g. the narrator of 'The Dead-Beat' is a soldier in the trenches.
onomatopoeia	A word that **sounds like** the thing it's describing, e.g. "click" and "whistling" in 'Jumper'.
oxymoron	A phrase which appears to **contradict** itself, e.g. "A sight so touching in its majesty".
personification	Describing a nonliving thing as if it has **human thoughts** and **feelings**, or **behaves** in a human way, e.g. "The dark air carried my cry".
Petrarchan sonnet	A form of **sonnet** in which the first eight lines have a regular ABBA rhyme scheme and **introduce** a problem, while the final six lines have a different rhyme scheme and **solve** the problem.
plosive	A **short burst of sound** made when you say a word containing the letters b, d, g, k, p or t.
quatrain	A **four-line** stanza.
refrain	A **line** or **stanza** in a poem that is **repeated**. E.g. "Don't say I said to say it" in 'Don't Say I Said'.
rhetorical question	A **question** that doesn't need an answer, but is asked to **make** or **emphasise** a point.
rhyme scheme	A **pattern** of rhyming words in a poem. E.g. 'When You Are Old' has an **ABBA** rhyme scheme — this means that the **first** and **fourth** lines in each stanza rhyme, and so do the **second** and **third** lines.
rhyming couplet	A **pair of rhyming lines** that are next to each other, e.g. the last two lines of 'Eating Poetry'.
rhyming triplet	**Three rhyming lines** that are next to each other.
rhythm	A **pattern of sounds** created by the arrangement of **stressed** and **unstressed** syllables.
second person	When the narrator talks directly to **another person** using words like **"you"**.
sibilance	Repetition of 's' and 'sh' sounds, e.g. "she dusts the house, / sweeps".
simile	A way of describing something by **comparing** it to something else, usually by using the words "like" or "as", e.g. "like a cold grey sheet".
sonnet	A form of poem with **fourteen lines**, that usually follows a **clear rhyme scheme**. Sonnets are often used for love poetry.
stanza	A **group of lines** in a poem. Stanzas can also be called **verses**.
structure	The **order** and **arrangement** of ideas and events in a poem, e.g. how it begins, develops and ends.
syllable	A single **unit of sound** within a word. E.g. "all" has one syllable, "always" has two.
symbolism	When an object **stands for something else**. E.g. Blake's "Tyger" symbolises the whole of creation.
syntax	The **arrangement** of words in a sentence or phrase so that they make sense.
theme	An important **idea** or **topic** in a piece of writing. E.g. a poem could be based on the theme of love.
third person	When a poet writes about a character who **isn't** the speaker, using words like **"he"** or **"she"**.
tone	The **mood** or **feelings** suggested by the way the narrator **writes**, e.g. confident, thoughtful.
voice	The **personality** narrating the poem. Poems are usually written either using the poet's voice, as if they're speaking to you **directly**, or the voice of a **character**.
volta	A **turning point** in a poem, when the argument or tone **changes dramatically**.

Acknowledgements

We would like to thank the following copyright holders:

Cover quote from 'Composed Upon Westminster Bridge' by William Wordsworth

Cloud graphic on cover from Vecteezy.com/members/freevector

'Ninetieth Birthday' from Collected Poems: 1945-1990 *by R.S. Thomas, published by JM Dent, a division of The Orion Publishing Group, London.*

'My Grandmother' by Elizabeth Jennings, from The Puffin Book of Classic Verse *(Puffin Books, 1997).*

'Handbag' from Fifteen to Infinity *by Ruth Fainlight (Hutchinson, 1983), © Ruth Fainlight, 1983.*

'Jumper' published with permission from Tony Harrison © Tony Harrison

'The Dead-Beat' by Wilfred Owen, from Wilfred Owen: The War Poems *edited by Jon Stallworthy (Chatto & Windus, 1994).*

'The Bereavement of the Lion-Keeper' by Sheenagh Pugh from The Movement of Bodies *(Seren, 2005)*

'A century later' by Imtiaz Dharker from Over the Moon *(Bloodaxe Books, 2016). Reproduced with the permission of Bloodaxe Books. www.bloodaxebooks.com*

Natasha Trethewey, 'History Lesson' from Domestic Work. *Copyright © 1998, 2000 by Natasha Trethewey. Reprinted with the permission of The Permissions Company, LLC on behalf of Graywolf Press, Minneapolis, Minnesota, graywolfpress.org*

'Eating Poetry' from SELECTED POEMS *by Mark Strand, copyright © 1979, 1980 by Mark Strand. Used by permission of Alfred A. Knopf, an imprint the Knopf Doubleday Publishing Group, a division of Penguin Random House LLC. All rights reserved.*

'Volumes' taken from Her Book, Poems 1988-98 *© Jo Shapcott (Faber and Faber Ltd, Dec 2010)*

'Echo' by Walter de la Mare, by kind permission of The Literary Trustees of Walter de la Mare and The Society of Authors as their representative.

Jennifer Copley: 'At Sea'. By kind permission of Jennifer Copley.

'Don't Say I Said' from Pessimism for Beginners *by Sophie Hannah (Carcanet Press Limited, 2007)*

'Flowers' from Serious Concerns *by Wendy Cope (Faber and Faber Ltd, 2002)*

Every effort has been made to locate copyright holders and obtain permission to reproduce sources. For those sources where it has been difficult to trace the copyright holder of the work, we would be grateful for information. If any copyright holder would like us to make an amendment to the acknowledgements, please notify us and we will gladly update the book at the next reprint. Thank you.